TWENTY MILLION YANKEES
The Northern Home Front

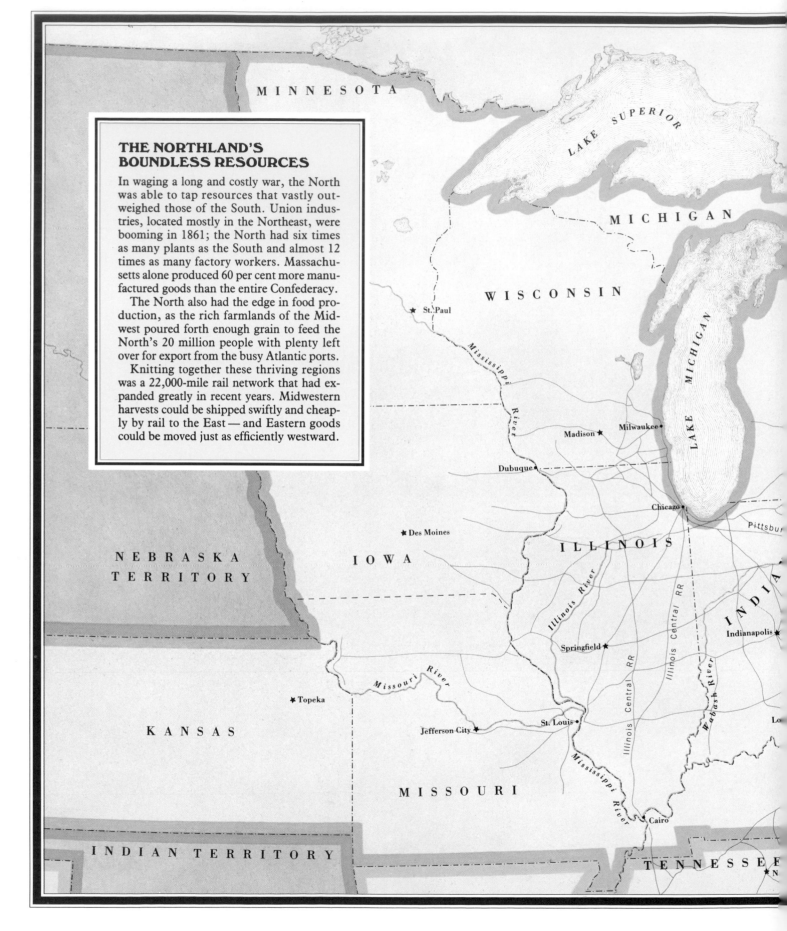

THE NORTHLAND'S BOUNDLESS RESOURCES

In waging a long and costly war, the North was able to tap resources that vastly outweighed those of the South. Union industries, located mostly in the Northeast, were booming in 1861; the North had six times as many plants as the South and almost 12 times as many factory workers. Massachusetts alone produced 60 per cent more manufactured goods than the entire Confederacy.

The North also had the edge in food production, as the rich farmlands of the Midwest poured forth enough grain to feed the North's 20 million people with plenty left over for export from the busy Atlantic ports.

Knitting together these thriving regions was a 22,000-mile rail network that had expanded greatly in recent years. Midwestern harvests could be shipped swiftly and cheaply by rail to the East — and Eastern goods could be moved just as efficiently westward.

MINNESOTA

LAKE SUPERIOR

MICHIGAN

WISCONSIN

★ St. Paul

Mississippi River

Madison ★   Milwaukee ●

LAKE MICHIGAN

Dubuque ●

Chicago ●

Pittsbur

ILLINOIS

★ Des Moines

NEBRASKA TERRITORY

IOWA

Illinois River

Illinois Central RR

INDIA

Indianapolis ●

Springfield ★

Illinois Central RR

Wabash River

Missouri River

KANSAS

★ Topeka

Jefferson City ★   St. Louis ●

Lo

Mississippi River

MISSOURI

INDIAN TERRITORY

Cairo ●

TENNESSE

★ N

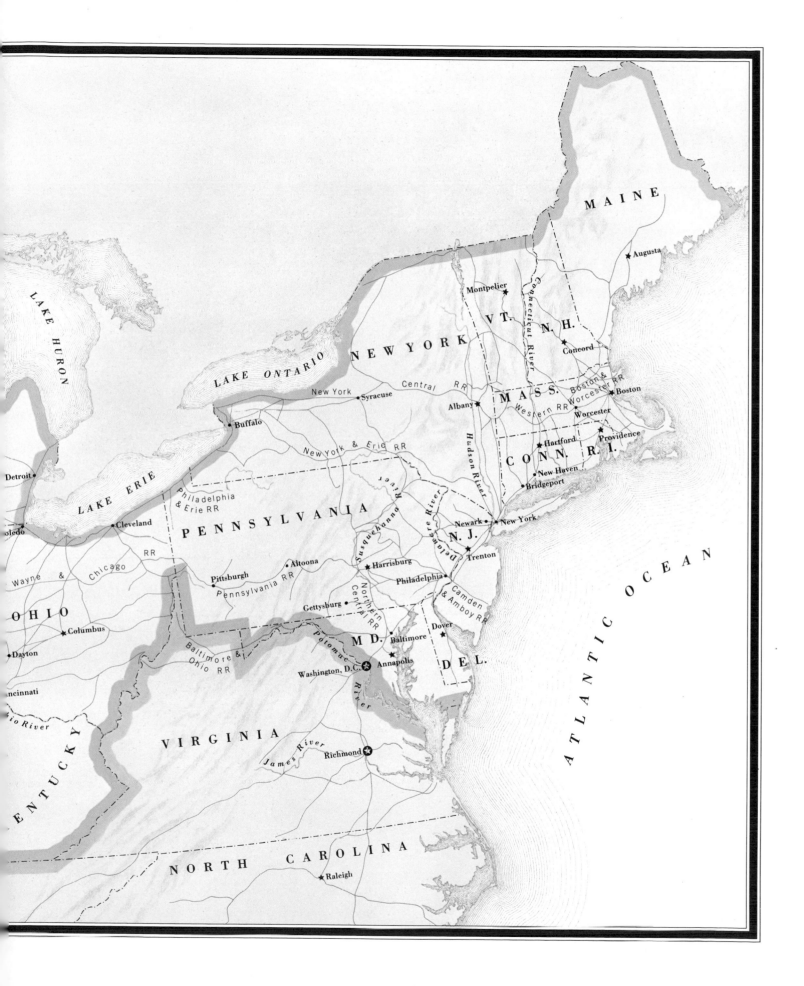

TIME®
LIFE
BOOKS

Other Publications:

THE NEW FACE OF WAR
HOW THINGS WORK
WINGS OF WAR
CREATIVE EVERYDAY COOKING
COLLECTOR'S LIBRARY OF THE UNKNOWN
CLASSICS OF WORLD WAR II
TIME-LIFE LIBRARY OF CURIOUS AND UNUSUAL FACTS
AMERICAN COUNTRY
VOYAGE THROUGH THE UNIVERSE
THE THIRD REICH
THE TIME-LIFE GARDENER'S GUIDE
MYSTERIES OF THE UNKNOWN
TIME FRAME
FIX IT YOURSELF
FITNESS, HEALTH & NUTRITION
SUCCESSFUL PARENTING
HEALTHY HOME COOKING
UNDERSTANDING COMPUTERS
LIBRARY OF NATIONS
THE ENCHANTED WORLD
THE KODAK LIBRARY OF CREATIVE PHOTOGRAPHY
GREAT MEALS IN MINUTES
PLANET EARTH
COLLECTOR'S LIBRARY OF THE CIVIL WAR
THE EPIC OF FLIGHT
THE GOOD COOK
WORLD WAR II
HOME REPAIR AND IMPROVEMENT
THE OLD WEST

This volume is one of a series that chronicles in full the events of
the American Civil War, 1861-1865.
Other books in the series include:

The Cover: New York City women on the small
reviewing stand present the colors to a newly
formed regiment, the 20th U.S. Colored Troops,
in a ceremony at Union Square in March 1864.

For information on and a full description of any of the Time-
Life Books series listed on this page, please call 1-800-621-
7026 or write:
Reader Information
Time-Life Customer Service
P.O. Box C-32068
Richmond, Virginia 23261-2068

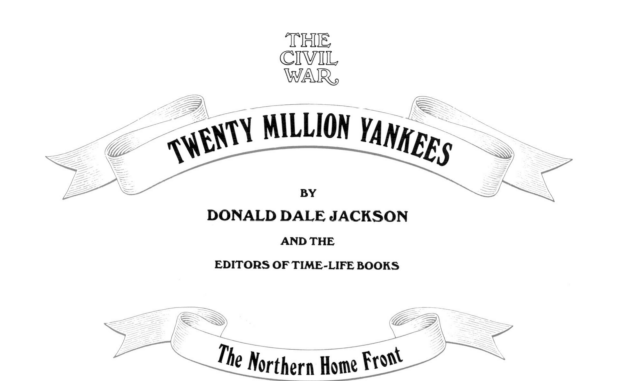

THE CIVIL WAR

TWENTY MILLION YANKEES

BY

DONALD DALE JACKSON

AND THE

EDITORS OF TIME-LIFE BOOKS

The Northern Home Front

TIME-LIFE BOOKS, ALEXANDRIA, VIRGINIA

Time-Life Books is a division of Time Life Inc.,
a wholly owned subsidiary of
THE TIME INC. BOOK COMPANY

TIME-LIFE BOOKS

PRESIDENT: Mary N. Davis

Managing Editor: Thomas H. Flaherty
Director of Editorial Resources: Elise D. Ritter-Clough
Director of Photography and Research:
John Conrad Weiser
Editorial Board: Dale M. Brown, Roberta Conlan,
Laura Foreman, Lee Hassig, Jim Hicks, Blaine
Marshall, Rita Thievon Mullin, Henry Woodhead

PUBLISHER: Robert H. Smith

Associate Publisher: Ann M. Mirabito
Editorial Director: Russell B. Adams, Jr.
Marketing Director: Anne C. Everhart
Production Manager: Prudence G. Harris
Supervisor of Quality Control: James King

Editorial Operations
Production: Celia Beattie
Library: Louise D. Forstall
Computer Composition: Deborah G. Tait
(Manager), Monika D. Thayer, Janet Barnes Syring,
Lillian Daniels

The Civil War
Series Director: Henry Woodhead
Designers: Cynthia T. Richardson, Herbert H. Quarmby
Series Administrator: Philip Brandt George

Editorial Staff for *Twenty Million Yankees*
Associate Editors: R. W. Murphy (text),
Jane N. Coughran (pictures)
Staff Writers: Jan Leslie Cook, Thomas H. Flaherty Jr.,
Thomas A. Lewis, David S. Thomson
Researchers: Stephanie Lewis, Gwen C. Mullen,
Andrea E. Reynolds (principals), Harris J. Andrews,
Susan V. Kelly
Copy Coordinator: Stephen G. Hyslop
Picture Coordinator: Betty H. Weatherley
Editorial Assistant: Audrey Prior Keir

Editorial Operations
Copy Chief: Diane Ullius
Editorial Operations Manager: Caroline A. Boubin
Production: Celia Beattie
Quality Control: James J. Cox (director)
Library: Louise D. Forstall

Correspondents: Elisabeth Kraemer-Singh
(Bonn); Maria Vincenza Aloisi (Paris); Ann Natanson
(Rome). Valuable assistance was also provided by
Carolyn Chubet (New York).

The Author:
Donald Dale Jackson, a former staff writer for *Life*, is the
author of several Time-Life books, including *Underground
Worlds* in the Planet Earth series, *Sagebrush Country* in
The American Wilderness series, and *The Aeronauts,
Flying the Mail* and *The Explorers* for The Epic of Flight.
He spent a year at Harvard University as a Nieman Fel-
low. Among his other books are *Judges*, a history of the
United States judicial system, and *Gold Dust*, a narrative
history of the California gold rush.

The Consultants:
Colonel John R. Elting, USA (Ret.), a former Associate
Professor at West Point, is the author of *Battles for Scandi-
navia* in the Time-Life Books World War II series and of
*The Battle of Bunker's Hill, The Battles of Saratoga, Mili-
tary History and Atlas of the Napoleonic Wars* and *American
Army Life.* Co-author of *A Dictionary of Soldier Talk*, he is
also editor of the three volumes of *Military Uniforms in
America, 1755-1867*, and associate editor of *The West Point
Atlas of American Wars.*

William A. Frassanito, a Civil War historian and lecturer
specializing in photograph analysis, is the author of two
award-winning studies, *Gettysburg: A Journey in Time* and
*Antietam: The Photographic Legacy of America's Bloodiest
Day*, and a companion volume, *Grant and Lee, The Virginia Campaigns.* He has also served as chief consultant to the
photographic history series *The Image of War.*

Les Jensen, Director of the Second Armored Division
Museum, Fort Hood, Texas, specializes in Civil War arti-
facts and is a conservator of historic flags. He is a contribu-
tor to *The Image of War* series, consultant for numerous
Civil War publications and museums, and a member of
the Company of Military Historians. He was formerly Curator of the U.S. Army Transportation Museum at Fort
Eustis, Virginia, and before that Curator of the Museum
of the Confederacy in Richmond, Virginia.

Michael McAfee specializes in military uniforms and has
been Curator of Uniforms and History at the West Point
Museum since 1970. A fellow of the Company of Military
Historians, he coedited with Colonel Elting *Long Endure:
The Civil War Years*, and he collaborated with Frederick
Todd on *American Military Equipage.* He is the author of
Artillery of the American Revolution, 1775-1783, and has
written numerous articles for *Military Images Magazine.*

James P. Shenton, Professor of History at Columbia University, is a specialist in 19th Century American political
and social history, with particular emphasis on the Civil
War period. He is the author of *Robert John Walker* and
Reconstruction South.

Library of Congress Cataloguing in Publication Data
Jackson, Donald Dale, 1935-
    Twenty million Yankees.
    (The Civil War)
    Bibliography: p.
    Includes index.
    1. United States — History — Civil War, 1861-1865.
I. Time-Life Books.   II. Title.   III. Series.
E456.J33 1985   973.7   84-28030
ISBN 0-8094-4752-5
ISBN 0-8094-4753-3 (lib. bdg.)

CONTENTS

At Arms in the Nation's Capital

When the War erupted in the spring of 1861, Washington, D.C., was as unprepared for the conflict as the rest of the Union. Scarcely 60 years old, the capital of the nation remained a small, unfinished city of 63,000 people. Only a handful of government buildings had been erected; the Capitol itself was incomplete. The few clusters of fine houses were surrounded by shantytowns and open fields. A newspaperman wrote that in wet weather the unpaved streets became "canals of liquid mud" full "of garbage, refuse and trash."

It fell to this scruffy, half-built capital to serve as the nerve center of the entire Union war effort, and as supply depot for the Federal armies fighting in the East. Washington became a huge, bustling military camp. Troops were everywhere, drilling, standing guard at public buildings, and moving through the city in long columns toward the Potomac bridges and the Virginia battlefront. Artillery jammed the streets, as did immense droves of cattle — army rations on the hoof.

The city also became a vast infirmary for the sick and wounded streaming back from encampments and battlefields. At one time in 1862, more than 50,000 men lay in the city's 60 or so improvised hospitals, a grim reminder to Washingtonians of the War's terrible human cost. Those hospitals, wrote poet Walt Whitman, who served in the area as a volunteer nurse, contained "the marrow of the tragedy."

Top-hatted members of the so-called Frontier Guard, a group of civilians hastily recruited to protect the President, form ranks on the White House lawn in April 1861. Washington's garrison was so small at the War's outset that several such temporary units were organized to guard the city.

New cannon and limbers await shipment on the grounds of Washington Arsenal, the Union's largest arms depot. The slope-sided sheds were built to contain various supplies; vast amounts of weapons and ammunition were made and stored in the brick buildings beyond.

Nine teams of oxen haul a 25-ton, 15-inch Rodman gun, the heaviest artillery piece used in the War, past the corner of 15th Street and Pennsylvania Avenue. Such heavy traffic cracked and ruined the city's few paved streets.

Cattle graze near a noisome canal on land that would become Washington's handsome Mall after the War. The porticoed Treasury Building, which was pressed i

ice as a barracks early in the conflict, is at upper right. The White House rises above the trees at center.

The officers of a civilian guard
unit composed of U.S. Treasury
clerks line up for an 1865 photograph with the unfinished Washington Monument in the background.

Their arms stacked, troops stand at ease on the
lawn before the east portico of the Capitol. Lincoln
insisted that work on the building continue despite
the expense and the wartime shortages. "It is a
sign," he said, "we intend the Union shall go on."

The barracks-like buildings of Harewood Hospital, one of Washington's many wartime infirmaries, stretch across farmland owned by the wealthy banker W. W. Corcoran, an antiwar Democrat who moved to England at the start of the conflict. Corcoran's downtown art gallery was commandeered by the Quartermaster Corps.

Maimed soldiers and others in nee gather outside the U.S. Christi Commission in downtown Washin ton. Standing with them are sor of the clergymen and volunteers w ran the charitable institutio

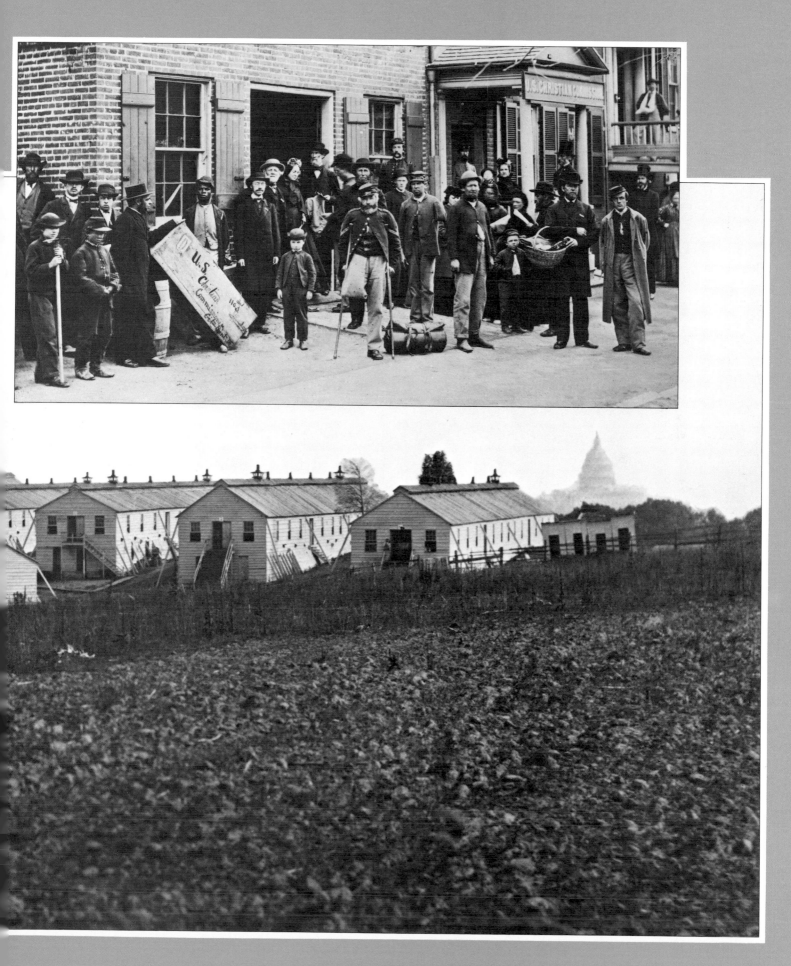

A soldier practices his marksmanship from a rocky promontory while others lounge about on Mason's Island in the Potomac. In the background the Aqueduct Bri

ans the river below the buildings of Georgetown College. A ferry connected Mason's Island with Georgetown's port, seen through the trees at right.

Fissures of Dissent

"The country is tired and sick of the war and longing for peace. I fear that the draft, the tax, the lack of victories, the discontent with the Cabinet and the other influences that are swelling the tide of hostility to the Administration will overbear it. In that event we should speedily have disunion and ruin."

HENRY J. RAYMOND, EDITOR OF THE NEW YORK *TIMES*

1

On a Saturday morning in August of 1861 — when North and South had been at war for four months — a group of citizens in Stepney, Connecticut, met on the village green under a white banner bearing the single word "Peace." They were assembled to protest what they called "the unrighteous war."

As the main speaker stepped forward, a column of carriages, horsemen and shouting pedestrians appeared over a rise on the road from Bridgeport. The newcomers were supporters of the War — including volunteers for the Connecticut militia who had been discharged recently after serving a three-month tour of duty. The two groups closed and scuffled. The white flag was torn down, and the peace faction fled the field. The triumphant volunteers returned to Bridgeport. There they marched on the office of the Bridgeport *Farmer*, known for its Southern sympathies, and destroyed the presses.

Such turbulent scenes were repeated throughout the North in the early months of the Civil War. They were testimony to a simple, if ill-perceived, truth: The Yankee nation did not speak with one voice — as the South and Europe sometimes assumed that it did — or act with one intention. The people of this diverse land could not agree on why they had gone to war — or whether they should be warring with the South at all.

To most Northerners, state and regional loyalties were far more compelling at the outbreak of war than the pull of nationhood.

Moreover, the North — much more than the agrarian South — was a land in rapid transition. While the South had change forced upon it by war, the North was in the full flux of change before the first shot was fired.

In 1860, the North's manufactured products had for the first time surpassed in value the rich flow of produce from its farms. Mechanization and mass production were accelerating the growth of both agriculture and manufacturing. New industries were springing up that were national in scope.

The North's population was still predominantly rural, but it was shifting to the cities. And foreign immigration was creating social problems that the native-born Protestant majority had never encountered before.

The War had the effect of increasing tensions in the region even as it brought many Northerners closer together. Some in the North simply abhorred the War and showed no reluctance to express their view. Volatile issues such as conscription and emancipation stirred further passion and fueled such protest that the government felt compelled to restrict civil liberties and define new limits of dissent. But at the same time, Northerners of diverse backgrounds found themselves bound together in wartime charitable efforts, or touched by the common empathy of those whose sons and husbands were risking their lives to fight for the Union.

With twice the population of the South and more than three times as much industry,

In a patriotic poster displayed early in the Civil War, a militant Columbia carries a flag whose 34 stars proclaim the ideal of an unbroken Union. President Lincoln insisted that the stars representing the seceded states not be removed from the national flag.

GOD, OUR COUNTRY AND LIBERTY.!!

THE SPIRIT OF '61.

the North had the latent strength to triumph in the War, and many of its citizens expected swift victory. But as the conflict dragged on, people asked if the Union had the will to win. In the face of battlefield defeats, many questioned whether the volatile electorate that had put Lincoln into office would continue to support him.

In the end — thanks in part to Lincoln's political genius — the sense of nationhood would prevail. The voices of dissent never fell silent, and the questioning of aims never ceased. But Northerners gradually found in the ideal of union a principle by which they could transcend their differences.

The land that went to war was a patchwork of ethnic groups. Of the 20 million people inhabiting the North at the time, about a

fifth were foreign-born. The vast majority of these came from Ireland, Germany or Great Britain. But a considerable number immigrated from the Scandinavian countries and Holland, and a few came from other countries of northwestern Europe. There was also a trickle from central and southern Europe — most notably from Poland and Italy. All told, immigration climbed during the war years to a level of about 250,000 annually. Among the newcomers were a certain number of undesirables — "the dregs and feculence of every land," a New York welfare agency labeled them — but most of the immigrants were responsible workingmen between the ages of 15 and 40, possessed of skills the Northern economy badly needed.

For the most part, the immigrants stuck together: A section of Cincinnati known as *Über dem Rhein* ("Across the Rhine") was distinguished by German-language signs, German beer and sausage and such a profusion of German-style clothing that a visitor thought he was walking a German street.

Slightly less than 1 per cent of the North's population was black. These "proscribed pariah people," as the English journalist Edward Dicey called them, were clustered mainly in tenements in the big cities. Largely restricted to the most menial jobs, they were a source of discord and embarrassment to Northern society. "The truth is," wrote Dicey, "the negroes, slave or free, are a race apart, in both North and South."

Three fourths of the North's population in 1860 lived on farms or in small towns, and more than half the gainfully employed worked the land. The Great Lakes region, the Mississippi Valley and the lands beyond were experiencing rapid population growth: The mineral-rich Colorado Territory, for example, more than tripled in population — from 32,000 to 100,000 — during the War.

At the same time, urban growth began to accelerate, mainly because of immigration from abroad and a counterflow of population from the poorer rural areas to the cities, where new jobs were being generated by the War. The population of Chicago nearly doubled during the conflict, while that of San Francisco grew by a third in just two years. A survey taken in New York showed that the state's larger communities were steadily gaining in population while most of the smaller ones were declining — a pattern that was repeated throughout the East.

The contrasts between rural and urban life were becoming starker. In the East, the life of the farmer had not changed in generations. According to an 1864 account in the magazine *Country Gentleman*, a typical New Hampshire farm comprised anywhere from 100 to 200 acres of woods, rough pasture land and tillable soil. The farmer kept perhaps 20 head of cattle, plus a few pigs and sheep. He raised corn, potatoes, oats and rye, butchered his stock for meat and churned his own butter. Salt meat and potatoes were the daily fare, with fresh meat a rare treat. The farmer sold timber from his woodlands and apples from his orchard. The

Remnants of an angry mob mill about the intersection of Water and Wall Streets in Bridgeport, Connecticut, after sacking the editorial offices of the pro-Southern *Farmer*. The rioters opened upstairs shutters to hurl out printing equipment, type cases and paper into the street below.

whole family pitched in to do the chores and harvest the crops. "So the generations go," observed *Country Gentleman*.

The departure of tens of thousands of farm boys for the War changed the placid shared routine of many farms. And *Country Gentleman* noted another fundamental and lasting change in rural life: On one farm after another, young men were leaving to try their luck in the West, or in the cities.

The flow of immigrant and native-born labor into the cities was transforming the nature of urban life as well. The newcomers propelled the cities into spasms of construction. Chicago, a guidebook noted, was evolving "from a condition of bottomless mud to pavements, and from the era of wooden shanties to permanent and costly buildings." In Chicago as elsewhere, new churches, hotels and civic structures rose on hundreds of downtown streets. But many workers, in the great cities as well as the grimy mill towns, lived in squalor in overcrowded tenements.

A social agency counted 401,000 tenement dwellers in New York in 1863, a number constituting nearly half the city's population. Virtually every Northern city had acres of dreary tenements squatting in the lee of factories. Life in those shelters was miserable and dangerous. The officers of the Russian fleet, visiting New York in 1863, were so touched by the plight of the slum dwellers that they donated $4,760 of their own money to help them buy fuel for their stoves.

While the well-to-do enjoyed such recent innovations as central heating and hot and cold running water, the poor were crowded eight and 10 to a single rancid room; outside the tenement was a trench a foot or two deep for a toilet. "The rags that cover the floor in lieu of a carpet reek with filth," a New York public health committee reported. "The bed clothing is often little better." The alleys between the tenements were "unventilated, unlighted holes." Refuse of all kinds — dead animals, factory waste, sewage — littered the fetid streets.

The miasmic conditions bred smallpox, typhus and other illnesses. Twelve thousand cases of typhoid fever were reported in New York in one year. In the single month of August 1864, about 1,700 infants died there from disease. In Washington, a city crowded to the bursting point during the War, an outbreak of smallpox affected untold thousands of people — many of them black refugees living in squalid camps on the outskirts. In their ignorance, slum dwellers passed on the disease by selling the clothes of the dead to second-hand dealers. The exact scale of the epidemic was unknown, for many cases went unreported, but the records show that at one point there were 1,000 smallpox victims in a single Washington hospital.

Such conditions spawned not only disease but a great deal of crime and violence. Rioting, sparked by ethnic tensions and labor disagreements, was commonplace. In cities where Irish immigration was heavy, the authorities blamed outbursts on the fact that the Irish had a long history of political upheaval. This was true — though the sorry lot of the Irish immigrants was reason enough for unrest.

Genuine political dissent during the War was not the product of the cities, however, or of any particular urban group. It came instead out of the Midwest — and particularly from the states of Ohio, Illinois and Indiana.

The hardscrabble farmland across the Midwest's southern tier of states was home to thousands of people born in the South —

A crowd gathers in Ann Arbor, Michigan, on the first day of war to hear a speech by University of Michigan President Henry Tappan. The citizens adopted a resolution to "stand by the President of the United States" and to organize military companies "in order to be ready to meet a draft."

many of them engaged in the lucrative trade that moved up and down the Ohio, Wabash and Illinois Rivers. For both practical and sentimental reasons, most of these people were bitterly opposed to the Union's war effort. Mustering their considerable resources, they mounted a sustained protest movement that produced most of the renowned antiwar leaders. Newspaper readers across the North became familiar with the outcries of men like Indiana Congressman Daniel Voorhees (known as "the Tall Sycamore of the Wabash"), Ohio Congressman Alexander Long, and fiery editors Dennis Mahony of Iowa, Samuel Medary of Ohio and Marcus Mills "Brick" Pomeroy of Wisconsin. But the man who would become the most passionate and visible spokesman for dissent was Democratic Congressman Clement L. Vallandigham of Dayton, Ohio.

Almost from the outset, the pressures of the War divided the Northern Democratic Party into two contentious factions. The central party organization remained in the hands of the so-called War Democrats, who generally supported President Lincoln's military efforts to defeat the Confederacy, but who opposed him on other vital issues, including the emancipation of the slaves. The Peace Democrats, on the other hand, denounced emancipation, came to regard Lincoln's prosecution of the War as a failure and demanded a negotiated peace with what one of them called "the injured, incensed, downtrodden people of the South."

Vallandigham was the most radical of the Peace Democrats, whose enemies labeled them Copperheads after the poisonous snake. The handsome and eloquent Congressman was 40 years old and serving his second term when the War began. A minis-

ter's son with a taste for martyrdom and a strong streak of dogmatic righteousness, he was temperamentally suited to be the leader of a dissenting cause.

"Valiant Val," as his friends called him, was a consistent champion of states' rights and an ardent Midwestern sectionalist. In his view slavery was a Constitutionally protected institution with which the federal government had no right to interfere. Beyond that, he expressed the fear that the Lincoln Administration by its war measures was centralizing the power of the government and subjugating the states. He wrote that he wanted to preserve "the Constitution as it is, the Union as it was" — meaning the prewar Union, in which slavery had its place. "I know that I am right," he said in April 1861, "and that in a little while the sober second thought of the people will dissipate the present sudden and fleeting public madness."

Vallandigham's frequent and fervid pronouncements provoked hostility from all quarters. Republicans and War Democrats alike assailed him as a "traitor" and a "friend of Jeff Davis" who was "worse than a Judas." Republicans circulated an unfounded story that a Confederate Army camp in Kentucky was named after him. Although the Administration ignored him, at least at first, his enemies in Dayton showed less restraint. When a Republican grocer he had long patronized called him a traitor and denied him credit, he threatened to thrash the man. The merchant pulled a pistol, and Vallandigham retreated to a millinery shop next door. A sympathizer once observed that he was "the most unpopular man in the North."

In 1861, Vallandigham sponsored a series of Congressional resolutions censuring the President for ordering what the Ohioan

Ohio Congressman Clement Vallandigham bitterly denounced the War, saying that it yielded only "defeat, debt, taxation, and sepulchres." His extreme views made him the hero of the Peace Democrats and a symbol of sedition for the rest of the North.

called the "illegal arrests" of dissidents, usurping the power of Congress to declare war and raise troops, and stifling free speech and the press. His resolutions were tabled amid muttered imprecations from his opponents. But while he was reviled in Washington, his fellow Ohio Peace Democrats followed his lead. A state convention dominated by the peace faction blamed the War on "fanatical agitators, North as well as South," and called for a national convention to resolve regional differences.

Vallandigham stunned Congress early in 1862 by introducing a bill to imprison the President. Campaigning for reelection that year, he spoke of martyrdom: "I may die for the cause, but the immortal fire shall outlast the humble organ which conveys it." He added that "the breath of liberty" would surely survive "the prophet" — as he had taken to calling himself. Although he was narrowly defeated for a third term, he continued to make blistering speeches. He said on one occasion that he would rather his "right arm were plucked from its socket and cast into eternal burnings" than that he should lend his support to the War.

In the spring of 1863 he was seeking the Democratic nomination for governor of Ohio when he ran afoul of General Ambrose Burnside. After his crushing defeat at Fredericksburg the previous December, Burnside had been given command of the Department of the Ohio, based in Cincinnati. Finding himself in a nest of Copperheads, the general issued an order in April stating that "treason" would not be tolerated in his department. When Vallandigham persisted in making inflammatory speeches, Burnside acted. On his orders, soldiers hammered on the door of Vallandigham's home in Dayton at 2 a.m. on May 5 and shouted that he was under arrest. When he refused to come to the door, the troops smashed it down and charged inside, where a somewhat bizarre conversation ensued. The officer in command called for "Mr. Vallan*dig*ham" — stressing the third syllable of the name — to come downstairs. "My name is not Vallan-*dig*ham," a voice replied testily. "I don't care how you pronounce it," the officer retorted. "You are my man."

The soldiers escorted the prisoner to a waiting train that carried him to Cincinnati, where he was held under guard. In a message he managed to smuggle out, he protested

Federal troops take Clement Vallandigham into custody after battering down the door to his home in Dayton, Ohio. The arrest so enraged his Democratic followers that mobs took to the streets and the Republican leaders of Dayton went into hiding.

that he had been imprisoned "for no other offense than my political opinions." When his friends in Dayton learned of his arrest, they rushed into the streets with torches and attacked and damaged the office of Dayton's Republican *Daily Journal*.

Vallandigham's widely publicized trial before a nine-man military commission began the next day, May 6. The defendant was charged with "publicly expressing sympathy for those in arms against the government of the United States and declaring disloyal sentiments and opinions." Vallandigham retorted: "I am a Democrat — for the Constitution, for law, for the Union, for liberty — this

is my only 'crime.'" The commission found him guilty and sentenced him to a military prison for the duration of the War.

Protests over the government's action came thick and fast. Democrats everywhere denounced the proceedings against Vallandigham, and those in Ohio unanimously nominated the prisoner for governor. In response to the protests, President Lincoln posed a disarming question: "Must I shoot a simple-minded soldier boy who deserts, while I must not touch a hair of the wily agitator who induces him to desert?" Anxious to reduce passions in the case and to avoid creating an antiwar martyr, the President then commuted Vallandigham's sentence to banishment to the South.

Vallandigham soon was aboard a Federal gunboat en route to Louisville, where he transferred to a train for Nashville and the battlefront beyond Murfreesboro, Tennessee. Union officers accompanied him past the picket lines under a flag of truce, but then had difficulty in finding a Confederate who would step forward and officially accept him. When finally a soldier approached, the officers discreetly retreated while Vallandigham recited a statement he had prepared. "I am a citizen of Ohio and of the United States," he informed the perplexed Confederate. "I am here within your lines by force and against my will. I therefore surrender myself to you as a prisoner of war."

For the next few weeks he was a man without a country, unwanted by either side. But in mid-June he sailed from Wilmington, North Carolina, on a blockade-runner bound for Bermuda; from there he went on to Canada. He would be heard from again before the guns were stilled, but he would no longer occupy center stage.

Vallandigham and other leading Copperhead spokesmen were insistently visible and vocal. But the secret pro-Southern society known as the Knights of the Golden Circle, or the KGC, caused Union leaders much more concern. The society was founded in 1854 to promote American expansion and the extension of slavery into Mexico and around the Gulf — thus the "golden circle." During the War, the KGC became a clandestine organization of Southern sympathizers concentrated in the Midwest. Though the Knights themselves never posed a military threat, they were widely believed to be active

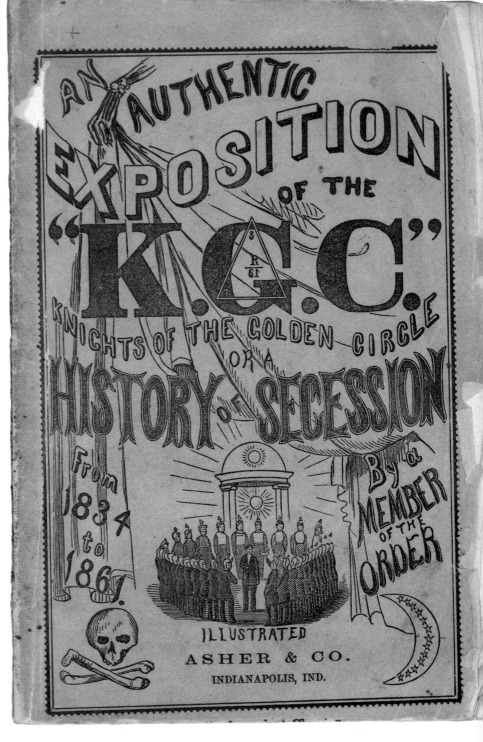

AN AUTHENTIC EXPOSITION OF THE "K.G.C." KNIGHTS OF THE GOLDEN CIRCLE OR A HISTORY OF SECESSION from 1834 to 1861. By a MEMBER OF THE ORDER

ILLUSTRATED
ASHER & CO.
INDIANAPOLIS, IND.

in gathering recruits and supplies for the Confederacy and in aiding Union deserters. The aura of mystery that cloaked their activities fostered a wealth of rumors: One concerned a plot to set fires simultaneously in New York, Philadelphia and Boston.

Dozens of KGC lodges, where members greeted each other with secret handshakes and performed elaborate rituals, were said to flourish in southern Indiana and Illinois. Other branches were reported in Michigan, Ohio, Iowa, California and elsewhere. In Illinois, the KGC was said to have a membership of 20,000. After an investigation, a federal grand jury in Indiana declared in August 1862 that the KGC rolls in that state included 15,000 members sworn "to resist the payment of the federal tax and to prevent enlistment in the army." The grand jury indicted 60 men on various treason and conspiracy charges. But government prosecutors were reluctant to pursue the matter — in part because of a fear of creating martyrs and in part because the cases were weak. Eventually, the indictments were quietly dropped.

In fact, little evidence of treasonable activity materialized in any of the states where the KGC was supposedly active. The government was not even able to determine the Knights' true strength. The real significance of the KGC was not that it undermined the Union war effort but that it helped create a climate of fear in which the restraint of civil rights became commonplace. Democrats charged that hysteria about KGC activities was pumped up by the government to give officials a freer hand in dealing with dissent.

The Lincoln Administration was plagued as well by the question of how to deal with the brutally outspoken Northern press. The normal level of editorial invective in the 19th Century was shrill, and it became even more so after the War began. Brick Pomeroy of the La Crosse, Wisconsin, *Democrat* insulted Lincoln at every turn, raging that he had "swapped the Goddess of Liberty for the pate and wool of a nigger." Samuel Medary of the Columbus, Ohio, *Crisis* called Lincoln a "half-witted usurper," while the Jerseyville, Illinois, *Democratic Union* said he was "a worse traitor than Jefferson Davis."

Such invective sometimes triggered a violent response. An angry crowd in Haverhill, Massachusetts, tarred and feathered an editor accused of sympathizing with secession, then forced him to apologize on his knees. Marauding bands of soldiers gutted the Franklin, Indiana, *Herald*, the Chester, Illinois, *Picket Guard* and many other papers.

The government had to determine when a free press abused its freedom. The case of the Newark *Evening Journal* was typical of the questions raised. Responding to Lincoln's call for a half million troops in 1863, the *Evening Journal* issued a provocative challenge: "Those who wish to be butchered will please step forward. All others will please stay at home and defy Old Abe and his minions to drag them from their families." Did this obstruct the draft? A federal judge thought so, and the editor was arrested, convicted and fined.

In another, much-publicized case, the New York *Daily News*, owned by the Copperhead Congressman Benjamin Wood, had to suspend publication for 18 months after it was barred from the mail by Postmaster General Montgomery Blair. Blair claimed for himself the authority to bar papers he deemed "insurrectionary or treasonable or in any degree inciting to treason or insurrec-

blished in 1861, this fictionalized osé of a pro-Southern secret soci-, the Knights of the Golden Circle, led fears of Confederate sedition he North. The cover shows an ate surrounded by Knights, along h a 13-starred crescent symboliz-the Confederacy and a skull signi-g death to abolitionists.

tion." During the War, more than 20 Northern and border state papers were suppressed by the government for varying periods.

The two-day shutdown of the Chicago *Times* in June 1863 was the most dramatic clash between the press and government authorities. Editor Wilbur Storey, enraged by the summary arrest in May of Vallandigham, charged the Administration in an editorial with abandoning law in favor of military despotism. Soon after the editorial appeared, General Burnside retaliated. He ordered the shutdown of the *Times*, Chicago's leading Democratic paper, for "repeated expressions of disloyal and incendiary sentiments."

But this time it was immediately clear that the blundering Burnside had gone too far.

While Storey obtained a court order delaying the shutdown, his staff managed to get out a partial press run before the troops arrived. Chicago's Democrats, a majority of the city's voters, took to the streets 20,000 strong to protest. Some urged a retaliatory attack on the Republican *Tribune*, a threat that was real enough for a New York reporter in Chicago to end his dispatch, "At this hour the *Tribune* still stands."

When a bipartisan group of civic leaders asked President Lincoln to rescind Burnside's order, he quickly did so. Secretary of

Tarred and feathered, the editor of a pro-Confederate weekly newspaper in Haverhill, Massachusetts, is being ridden through town on a rail. According to the Philadelphia *Inquirer*, he was forced to swear he would never again publish articles "against the North and in favor of secession."

In a contemporary cartoon, the ghostly finger of Secretary of State William Seward presses a bell — a reference to Seward's boast that with the ring of a bell he could send any citizen to jail. In the other panels, a hapless antiwar dissident is arrested in the dead of night, marched off to prison and incarcerated with the grieving figure of Liberty.

War Edwin Stanton then explained to the impulsive Burnside that "the irritation produced by such acts is likely to do more harm than the publication would do." The brief suppression proved to be a boon to the *Times*, which enjoyed an increase in circulation while remaining as belligerent as ever. Storey laid in a supply of muskets in case of further trouble. The next time General Burnside visited Chicago, the *Times* greeted him as "the butcher of Fredericksburg and attempted assassin of the liberty of speech."

Lincoln subsequently relaxed restraints on the press. As he instructed one of his generals: "You will only suppress newspapers when they may be working palpable injury to the military in your charge. In this you have a discretion to exercise with great caution, calmness, and forbearance."

Forbearance was conspicuously absent in the wave of 13,000 arrests made by Union officials between 1861 and 1863. On April 27, 1861, in response to secessionist activity in Maryland, Lincoln suspended the writ of habeas corpus along the vital Washington-Philadelphia lines of communication, permitting suspected subversives there to be detained without trial. Throughout that year internal security was in the hands of the State Department, under Secretary of State William Seward. He made no secret of his intentions: To send a suspect to jail, he boasted, he had only to ring a bell on his desk. The remark stirred a storm of protest — not because it was so arrogant but because it was so patently true. Hundreds of suspected spies and saboteurs, particularly in the border states, were summarily arrested.

In February 1862 responsibility for maintaining security in the Union was shifted to the War Department and Edwin Stanton. Arrests decreased for a time, but then picked up again during the summer of that year in response to increased Copperhead agitation following Union reverses on the battlefield. In August 1862, almost simultaneously with the announcement of a draft, a War Department order authorized the arrest of anyone who discouraged enlistments or who engaged in other "disloyal practices" against the United States.

Yet even that sweeping order seemed insufficient to Lincoln as opposition to the draft built up in the fall of 1862. On September 24 he extended his suspension of habeas corpus to include the whole of the North.

Officers were thus free to jail and hold suspects on almost any pretext.

In fact, the suspension merely gave official sanction to what everybody knew was already going on. Both before and after Lincoln's order, dissenters were dumped without due process into military compounds like New York's Fort Lafayette, Boston's Fort Warren or Washington's Old Capitol Prison — for offenses as wispy as "being a noisy secessionist" or "hurrahing for Jeff Davis." Maryland policemen whose loyalty was challenged were seized on the grounds that they contemplated "some purpose not known to the government" but presumed dangerous. A minister in occupied Alexandria, Virginia, was arrested for neglecting the prayer for the President prescribed in a church service. One southern Illinois marshal went out in a burst of patriotic zeal and arrested nearly 40 dissidents, including a Democratic Congressman and several judges.

While many arrests were impromptu affairs, others were carried out in response to warrants issued directly by the War Department. This was the case with Dr. Edson Olds, a 60-year-old Congressman from Lancaster, Ohio. After publicly criticizing Lincoln, Dr. Olds was routed out of bed on August 12, 1862, by soldiers who knocked down his bedroom door. He was then sent to Washington and imprisoned. An editor who protested the arrest of Olds was summoned by Governor David Tod and told to correct his thinking. When the editor objected, the governor declared, "I am to be the judge of what you may and may not publish, constitutions and laws notwithstanding."

Peppery Dennis Mahony, editor of the Dubuque *Herald*, was a prominent Peace Democrat. At 3:30 a.m. on August 14, 1862,

he was awakened by soldiers carrying a War Department warrant. Arrested, he was placed aboard a train for Washington. At a layover, Mahony was registering at a trackside hotel when the officer escorting him insisted that he record his destination. "Bound for hell," Mahony wrote, "sent there by the devil for speaking the truth."

A few days later, Mahony fetched up in the fetid Old Capitol Prison. Ten weeks passed without his being told the charges against him. Back in Dubuque, his paper crowed sarcastically: "Long live Abraham Lincoln, who gives us more liberty than we know what to do with." Assistant Secretary of War Peter Watson answered a demand for the release of Mahony and another editor by declaring, "Let them prove themselves innocent and they will be discharged."

Mahony and his cellmates helped pass the time each day by marching back and forth behind one of their fellow prisoners, an Illinois judge, while he led them in song. Mahony, nominated *in absentia* as the Democratic candidate in his Congressional district, was freed after signing a loyalty oath. Defeated in the race, he wrote a book about his imprisonment and sarcastically dedicated it to Secretary of War Stanton.

The high-handed arrests on vague or unstated charges outraged not only Democrats but many Republicans, among them New York lawyer and diarist George Templeton Strong. "Not one of the many hundreds illegally arrested and locked up for months has been publicly charged with any crime," he exclaimed. "All this is very bad — imbecile, dangerous, unjustifiable." Senator Lyman Trumbull of Illinois was no less impassioned. "The idea that the rights of the citizen are to be trampled upon and that he is to

In an allegorical painting done in 1862, the antiwar Copperheads of New York's Tammany Hall chain Abraham Lincoln to the Constitution as he attacks the Confederate dragon. The vision of Washington in flames in the background rebukes those who wished to fetter the President because he was stretching his Constitutional powers.

be arrested by military authority, without any regulation by law," Trumbull declared, was "monstrous in a free government."

Lincoln's right to suspend habeas corpus was challenged in the courts by a Maryland citizen arrested for pro-Confederate activities. Sitting as a circuit judge in the case, Chief Justice Roger Taney declared that the President lacked the proper authority. Lincoln ignored the ruling, citing the Constitutional provision that habeas corpus could be suspended "when in cases of rebellion or invasion the public safety may require it."

Yet Lincoln was troubled by the problem,

and he referred to it often. In general, he argued that the normal judicial system was not adequate to deal with rebellion. And he made a distinction between peacetime imprisonment, as punishment for crimes committed, and wartime imprisonment, which was, he argued, "not so much for what has been done, as for what probably would be done." Such detention, he stressed, was "preventive" rather than "vindictive."

It was a fine line he was drawing, and a dangerous one. For neither the Supreme Court nor the Congress was able to curb the President's power during the War. What saved the situation was the character of Lincoln himself — humane, compassionate and devoted to democracy. At his instigation, the government freed many political prisoners after the 1862 elections. The number of arrests dropped off sharply after the outburst provoked by the Vallandigham case in 1863.

The currents of dissent still flowed, however. On their return home, Dennis Mahony and many other political prisoners were greeted as heroes. A crowd estimated at 10,000 welcomed Dr. Olds back to Ohio.

The most volatile issue that divided the North was the question of slavery. At the outbreak of war, most Northerners were ambivalent about slavery and uneasy about discussing it openly. Many could identify with an assertion Lincoln had made before the War: "I confess I hate to see the poor creatures hunted down and caught and carried back to their stripes and unrequited toil, but I bite my lips and keep quiet."

When England's Edward Dicey toured the North in 1862, he found that there were plenty of voluble demagogues on both sides of the slavery question, but the man in the street remained reticent, reminding Dicey of the South American ruler who tried to banish cholera from his country by forbidding mention of its name. Slavery and abolition were on everybody's mind but "kept studi-

The North's Stinging Gadfly

A wag once said that Horace Greeley was "a self-made man who worshipped his creator." The self-esteem of America's most famous editor stemmed from his conviction that he and his paper, the New York *Tribune*, were the voices of America's destiny. His genius was that he made much of the country believe the same thing.

As one of the founders of the Republican Party, Greeley set himself up as an arbiter of war policy and a maker or breaker of generals and Presidents. In its heyday during the Civil War, his "Trib" in its various editions was seen each week by more than a million Americans and functioned almost as an organ of government. President Lincoln said the *Tribune's* support was worth 100,000 men, and Confederate officals studied it to fathom Northern intentions.

Born on a hardscrabble New Hampshire farm, the young Greeley apprenticed with a local printer before moving to New York and launching the *Tribune* in 1841, largely on borrowed capital. He defined his paper in terms of what he was against: "Anti-Slavery, Anti-War, Anti-Rum, Anti-Tobacco, Anti-Seduction." A born scold, he fulminated against the depravities of the city while describing them in sufficient detail to titillate "the virtuous and refined" to whom he said he was speaking. Urban poverty shocked him and turned him into a social reformer: Noting caustically that freedom for American labor meant "liberty to go barefoot," he became an early advocate of collective bargaining and government-supported unemployment relief.

Greeley's greatest asset was his own passionate, intemperate voice. Mixing idealism and practicality, he championed in print such causes as tax-supported public schools and free land distribution. Readers loved his crotchets (a cigar, he fumed, had "a fire at one end and a fool at the other") and his disdain for the mighty: "Congress did nothing yesterday, to speak of," read the whole of one of his Washington reports.

This idiosyncratic reformer was hobbled by neither consistency nor facts. He both extolled and distrusted the common man, praised and denounced Lincoln, and continually wavered in his support of the War. But he was resolute in his opposition to slavery and in his visionary faith in the American future. That faith, and the sense he conveyed to his readers that they had a share in its promise, made him a secular prophet for two generations of Americans.

Greeley's benign appearance, accentuated b trademark fringe of white hair, surprised read of his pugnacious editorials. Planter's hat atilt, often visited the *Tribune's* press room (rig

ously out of sight." Dicey concluded that most Yankees seemed to want an end to slavery, but they desired just as strongly to somehow "get rid of the Negro."

Blacks were disparaged as shiftless and inferior by all but the most enlightened whites in the North, and were subject to discriminatory laws throughout the Union. Indiana and Illinois had local statutes forbidding freedmen to take up residence, while only three states — Massachusetts, Maine and New Hampshire — permitted them to vote on a par with whites. Segregation was practiced in almost all Northern schools. The prejudice was at times expressed in violence. A black man who scuffled with an Irishman in

Milwaukee was later hauled out of his jail cell and lynched by a mob shouting, "Damn the niggers and abolitionists." Race riots erupted in 1862 between black and white laborers in Toledo and Cincinnati.

Lincoln's initial policy was to proceed slowly to bring about emancipation, for fear of losing the loyalty of the slaveholding border states. At first he proposed paying border state slaveholders a $400 compensation for each slave they freed, thus encouraging voluntary emancipation. To reduce fears of race mingling, he suggested resettling the ex-slaves outside the country, perhaps in Central America. Negro orator Frederick Douglass spoke for many blacks when he

spurned this idea. "Every fact in our circumstances here," he said, "marks us as a permanent element of the American people."

As the months passed, the sentiment of the Northern public toward blacks — and toward slavery — began to shift. To be sure, there were practical reasons for this. At the start of the War, when blacks formed volunteer companies and tried to enlist, they were rejected. But then the casualty tolls began to rise, and the Army began to experience difficulty in filling its ranks. One solution was to have blacks fight in their own cause. Sadly, those who advocated black enlistment were often just as bigoted as those who opposed it. Thus Governor Israel Washburn of Maine argued in December of 1862 that blacks should serve because it was time for "Sambo" to "save white boys."

Many Northerners shared this grudging acceptance of the blacks' role in the War. "Everybody here is coming over to the notion of enlisting the darkeys," wrote Captain John W. De Forest from a Union camp in Louisiana. He added that "even old Democrats" and the Irish "rank and file" were beginning to favor it.

The idea of emancipation was also becoming more familiar — and perhaps more acceptable. As early as October of 1861, a New York newspaper saw evidence of a change of attitude in the roaring crowds that greeted a parading Massachusetts regiment led by an avowed abolitionist. In December of that year, the fervent abolitionist Wendell Phillips, who had frequently been chased off lecture stages in the past, was surprised to hear himself cheered when he told a New York audience that "the bloodiest war that ever raged is infinitely better than the happiest slavery that ever fettered man into obedi-

ence." A month later, Ralph Waldo Emerson told a Washington gathering that included the President: "Emancipation is the demand of civilization. That is a principle; everything else is an intrigue."

Could civil war elevate the national conscience? George Richards, an outspoken Connecticut clergyman, contended that the War was making Americans less selfish. Even more important, he said, "we are beginning to realize that colored people, even, may have rights, inalienable rights, among which is liberty." He discerned an "increasing conscience on this subject."

The hanging of a slave ship captain in New York in February 1862, the first execution for slave trading in the nation's history, was seen by some as further evidence of a shift in public opinion. The captain, Nathaniel Gordon, had been captured off the African coast before the War and forced to return his cargo to Africa. Though federal laws against the slave trade had been on the books for years, they had rarely been enforced. But now, slavery was becoming the enemy.

In April 1862, Congress voted to abolish slavery in the District of Columbia. The act, which both houses approved by more than 2-to-1 majorities, resembled a plan Lincoln was unsuccessfully trying to sell to the border states: Slaveowners were to be compensated; the relocation of blacks to another country was to be encouraged. Among those voting against the measure was Clement Vallandigham, who identified it, correctly, as the first step in a grand "scheme of emancipation." Washington's blacks were now free to go into business, to work for the government — and to stay out past the hour set for them as a curfew. Congress soon established schools for the District's black children.

These portraits, published as *cartes de visites* under the title, "Slave Children of New Orleans," purported to show quadroon or octaroon children who had been freed. Abolitionists thought the white appearance of the children made them more effective as antislavery propaganda. Proceeds from card sales went into an education fund for blacks.

Freedmen and abolitionists throughout the North celebrated the emancipation of the capital's slaves. Frederick Douglass hailed the development as "the first step toward a redeemed and regenerated nation." George Templeton Strong wrote: "Only the damnedest of 'damned abolitionists' dreamed of such a thing a year ago. John Brown's soul's a-marching on, with the people after it." A few months later Ohio Senator John Sherman discussed the issue in a letter to his brother, Union General William T. Sherman. "You can form no conception at the change of opinion here as to the Negro question," he wrote. "Men of all parties agree that we must seek the aid and make it the interests of the Negroes to help us." And he added: "I am prepared for one to meet the broad issue of universal emancipation."

In August, Horace Greeley published a long editorial in the New York *Tribune* en-

titled "The Prayer of Twenty Millions," which attacked Lincoln for the "seeming subserviency of your policy to the slave-holding, slavery-upholding interest." Greeley demanded immediate emancipation, as well as the use of Negro troops. The President, unknown to Greeley or the nation, had already made up his mind to free the slaves in the rebellious states under his authority as Commander in Chief. He could justify it as a war measure because it would harm the Confederate economy, and he believed it would also help the Union's cause abroad.

Lincoln had resolved to wait for an improvement in Northern military fortunes before announcing his decision, but Greeley's editorial gave him a chance to prepare the ground. "My paramount object in this struggle is to save the Union," he wrote Greeley in a letter subsequently published in the *Tribune*. "If I could save the Union without

LIBERTY
PROCLAMATION OF EMANCIPATION
Whereas, On the Twenty Second day of September in the year of our Lord one thousand eight hundred and sixty two, a Proclamation was issued by the President of the UNITED STATES containing among other things the following, to wit:
"That on the first day of January in the year of our Lord one thousand eight hundred and sixty three, all persons held as SLAVES within any STATE or designated part of a STATE, the people whereof shall then be in Rebellion against the UNITED STATES, shall be thenceforth and FOREVER FREE and the Executive Government of the UNITED STATES including the military and naval authorities thereof, will recognize and maintain the FREEDOM of such persons, and will do no act or acts to repress such persons or any of them, in any efforts they may make for their actual FREEDOM.
That the Executive will, on the first day of January aforesaid, by Proclamation, designate the STATES, and parts of STATES if any, in which the people therein respectively shall then be in Rebellion against the UNITED STATES, and the fact that any STATE or the people thereof shall on that day be in good faith represented in the Congress of the UNITED STATES by members chosen thereto at elections wherein a majority of the qualified voters of such STATE, shall have participated, shall, in the absence of strong countervailing testimony be deemed conclusive evidence that such STATE, and the people thereof are not then in Rebellion against the UNITED STATES.
Now therefore, I, ABRAHAM LINCOLN, President of the UNITED STATES, by virtue of the power in me vested as Commander in Chief of the Army and Navy of the UNITED STATES in time of actual armed Rebellion against the authority and Government of the UNITED STATES, and as a fit and necessary war measure for suppressing said Rebellion, do on this first day of January, in the year of our Lord one thousand eight hundred and sixty three, and in accordance with my purpose so to do publicly proclaim for the full period of one hundred days from the day of the first above-mentioned order, and designate as the STATES, and parts of STATES wherein the people thereof respectively are this day in Rebellion against the UNITED STATES the following, to wit: ARKANSAS, TEXAS, LOUISIANA, (except the Parishes of St. Bernard, Plaquemines, Jefferson, St. John, St. Charles, St. James, Ascension, Assumption, Terre Bonne, La Fourche, St. Mary, St. Martin, and Orleans, including the City of New Orleans,) MISSISSIPPI, ALABAMA, FLORIDA, GEORGIA, SOUTH CAROLINA, NORTH CAROLINA, AND VIRGINIA, (except the forty eight counties designated as WEST VIRGINIA, and also the counties of Berkeley, Accomac, Northampton, Elizabeth City, York, Princess Ann, and Norfolk, including the cities of Norfolk and Portsmouth,) and which excepted parts are for the present left precisely as if this Proclamation were not issued.
And by virtue of the power and for the purpose aforesaid, I do order and declare that all persons held as SLAVES within said designated STATES and parts of STATES are, and henceforward SHALL BE FREE, and that the Executive Government of the UNITED STATES including the Military and Naval Authorities thereof will recognize and maintain the FREEDOM of said persons.
And I hereby enjoin upon the people so declared to be FREE to abstain from all violence, unless in necessary self defence, and I recommend to them that in all cases when allowed, they labor faithfully for reasonable wages.
And I further declare and make known that such persons of suitable condition will be received into the armed service of the UNITED STATES to garrison forts, positions, stations and other places, and to man vessels of all sorts in said service.
And upon this act, sincerely believed to be an act of Justice, warranted by the Constitution upon military necessity, I invoke the considerate Judgment of mankind, and the gracious favor of Almighty God.
In testimony whereof I have hereunto set my name and caused the seal of the UNITED STATES to be affixed.
[L. S.] Done at the City of Washington, this first day of January in the year of our Lord one thousand eight hundred and sixty three, and of the Independence of the UNITED STATES the eighty seventh.
By the President
William H. Seward
Secretary of State
A. Lincoln
MAX ROSENTHAL DEL. & LITH.
L. N. ROSENTHAL LITH. No 327 WALNUT St PHILA.
L. Franklin Smith, Publisher, 327, Walnut St. Philadelphia, Box 2423

freeing any slave I would do it, and if I could save the Union by freeing some and leaving others alone I would also do that. What I do about slavery, and the colored race, I do because I believe it helps to save the Union."

When General George McClellan's army repelled the Confederate advance into Maryland at Antietam Creek on September 17, the President decided that the time had come. The announcement appeared in newspapers six days later. As of January 1, 1863, it read, "all persons held as slaves within any state, or designated part of a state, the people whereof shall then be in rebellion against the United States, shall be then, thenceforward, and forever free."

Significantly, Lincoln characterized the proclamation as "warranted by the Constitution upon military necessity" — thus tacitly acknowledging that it was an unusual use of the President's powers. To Treasury Secretary Salmon P. Chase, the President conceded that "the original proclamation has no legal justification, except as a military measure." Moreover, it announced no real change in war aims. Since it implied that slavery was permissible in nonrebellious states, it left open the possibility that the Southern states could retain slavery if they simply returned to the Union. But it quickly became apparent that the actual wording of the proclamation was less important than the effect it had on public opinion. Both friends and foes of the Administration took it to mean that henceforth the Union was waging war against slavery.

Critics on both sides immediately opened fire. Radical abolitionists contended that the proclamation was inadequate because it ignored the border states. Copperheads argued that it would harden Southern determination and eventually propel millions of blacks into competition with Northern workingmen.

Cautious and constrained in its language, Lincoln's proclamation lacked the scope and grandeur that many of its supporters thought the occasion demanded. In fact, it would take three more years and a Constitutional amendment before slavery in the United States was formally and finally at an end. But if the Emancipation Proclamation was "a poor document," as Massachusetts Governor John Andrew said, it was also "a mighty act." In recognition of that fact, Ralph Waldo Emerson and many other prominent Massachusetts abolitionists attended a "grand jubilee concert" at Boston's Music Hall on January 1, the day the proclamation took effect. Near the end of the program a man stepped onstage to announce that the word had arrived: Emancipation was now official. The crowd began a rhythmic chant for Harriet Beecher Stowe, the author of *Uncle Tom's Cabin,* who rose from her seat in the balcony and bowed shyly.

The night before in Washington, hundreds of black men and women had gathered at a barracks, where they prayed and sang and took turns talking about their experiences as slaves. On New Year's Day they rejoiced quietly, fearful that too much jubilation might draw an angry crowd. Their fears were realistic enough, for it would soon become clear that a mere proclamation could not overnight abolish all the tensions and hatreds that convulsed the North. But in the minds of many, the proclamation helped elevate the moral tone of the Northern cause. It provided a purpose worthy of the Union's best aspirations and its remarkable energies.

The Turbulent Metropolis

Nowhere was the prospect of the Civil War dreaded more deeply than in New York, the nation's largest city. No Northern city had closer ties to the South or greater reason for maintaining the peace.

New York in 1861 was a teeming metropolis of 816,000 citizens, growing too fast for its own good. A place of dramatic extremes, it had the broadest avenues and the most congested traffic, the finest mansions and grimmest slums, the most articulate civic leaders and most brazen corruption of any city in America.

For New Yorkers, Southern secession was a painful test of both patriotism and pocketbook. Wall Street was the South's broker and banker; most manufactured goods bound for the South passed through the port of New York. The mere thought of losing Southern markets — and the $300 million in credit that Southerners ultimately defaulted on — caused businessmen to tremble and scores of firms to collapse.

New York State had abolished slavery early in the century, yet the city remained a hotbed of proslavery sentiment. Meetings of abolitionists routinely were broken up by mobs. Within the city's polyglot population a brutal rivalry festered between the immigrant Irish and free blacks, who lived side by side in hard neighborhoods such as the Lower East Side's Five Points and competed for the same bottom-rung jobs. The Irish feared that emancipation would free millions of blacks willing to work for cheaper wages than they themselves were.

New York was overwhelmingly Democratic, and most of its 13 daily newspapers opposed President Lincoln's policies. Yet the Confederate attack on Fort Sumter in April of 1861 triggered a profound change in the public mood. Almost overnight, a majority of New Yorkers rallied to a single cry: "Preserve the Union — at any cost!"

The cost would prove to be high, and not just in money. Heeding Lincoln's call to arms, the city raised more than 50 regiments by the end of 1861. Nearly 1,000 of the Federal casualties at Bull Run that summer were New Yorkers — a token of further sacrifices to be made by the sons of the city.

Sailing ships and steamers ply the sheltered waters of New York's East River in this view looking westward toward the city's steepled skyline.

Horse-drawn wagons and carriages stream up and down Broadway, a bustling commercial artery four miles long, and flanked by buildings up to six stories tall.

Merchant ships from around the globe crowd the docks of New York City's waterfront. Cargo in the foreground awaits shipment to Washington.

Mobilizing a Great Port for War

The fortunes of New York were built on seagoing trade. Through its great natural harbor flowed one third of the nation's exports and two thirds of its imports.

The South as well as the North depended on New York as a hub of trade: More cotton moved through New York than any other Atlantic port. So vital was such traffic that in January of 1861, as civil war appeared imminent, Mayor Fernando Wood urged that New York declare itself a free city and continue doing business with both sides.

The mayor's proposal was brushed aside, and mobilization soon stretched the port's capacity to new limits. A torrent of men and matériel funneled through New York on the way to war. Exports of grain from the Midwest and petroleum from Pennsylvania more than made up for the loss of cotton.

New York's faithfulness to the Union embittered the city's Southern friends. "We could not have believed," complained the Richmond *Dispatch*, "that the city of New York, which has been enriched by Southern trade, would one day be converted into our bitterest enemy."

En route to war in April 1861, artillerymen load their munitions aboard the chartered steamship *Atlantic* at a covered Hudson River dock.

43

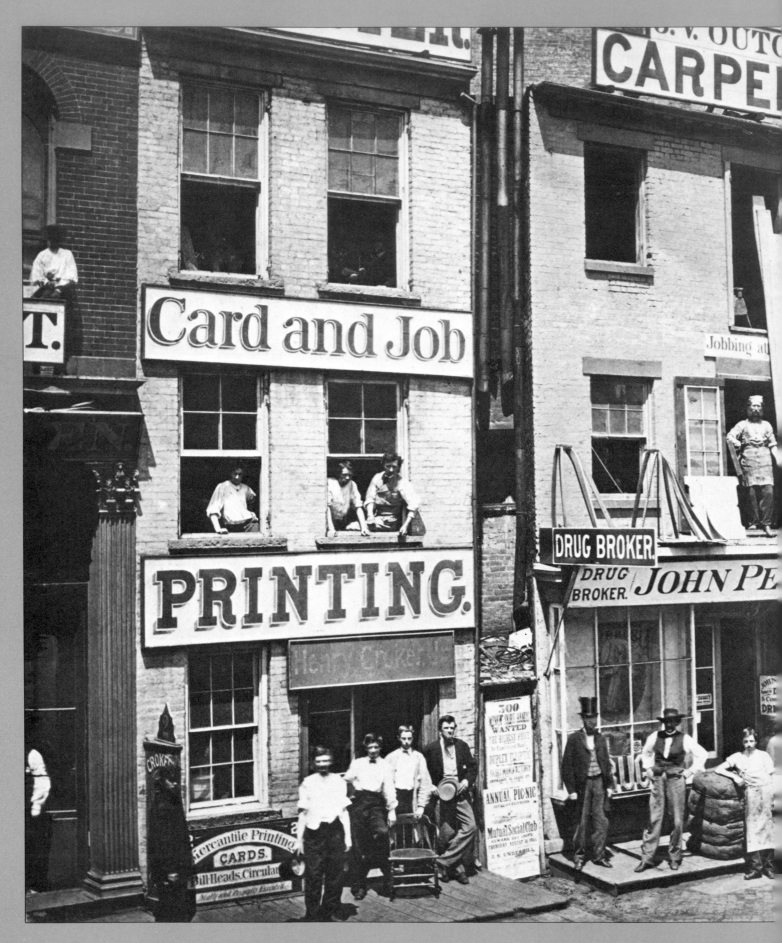

Businesses Buoyed by Greenbacks

Merchants with businesses both large and small formed the backbone of New York, and they were among the first to rally to the Union cause. "We are either for the country or for its enemies," declared the president of the Chamber of Commerce. A committee of volunteer businessmen, set up in 1861, led a drive to arm and clothe newly raised Federal regiments, provide relief for the families of soldiers, and send supplies to Army hospitals.

The commercial crisis that accompanied the opening of hostilities proved short-lived, and by 1862 New York business was thriving — especially after the federal government put millions of paper dollars, called greenbacks, into circulation for the first time.

Jobs were abundant, but wartime inflation brought strife and hardship for some New Yorkers. The price of food, coal and other necessities rose twice as fast as wages, prompting workers to organize for better conditions. Dockworkers struck in 1863 and won a pay increase to two dollars a day. That same year, store clerks joined forces in the Early Closing Movement and achieved a reduction in their work week — from 80 hours to 68.

Tradesmen turn out to have their picture taken in 1865 in front of their well-marked shops on Hudson Street. The swinging doors at lower right open into O'Brien's Sample Room, one of New York City's several hundred saloons.

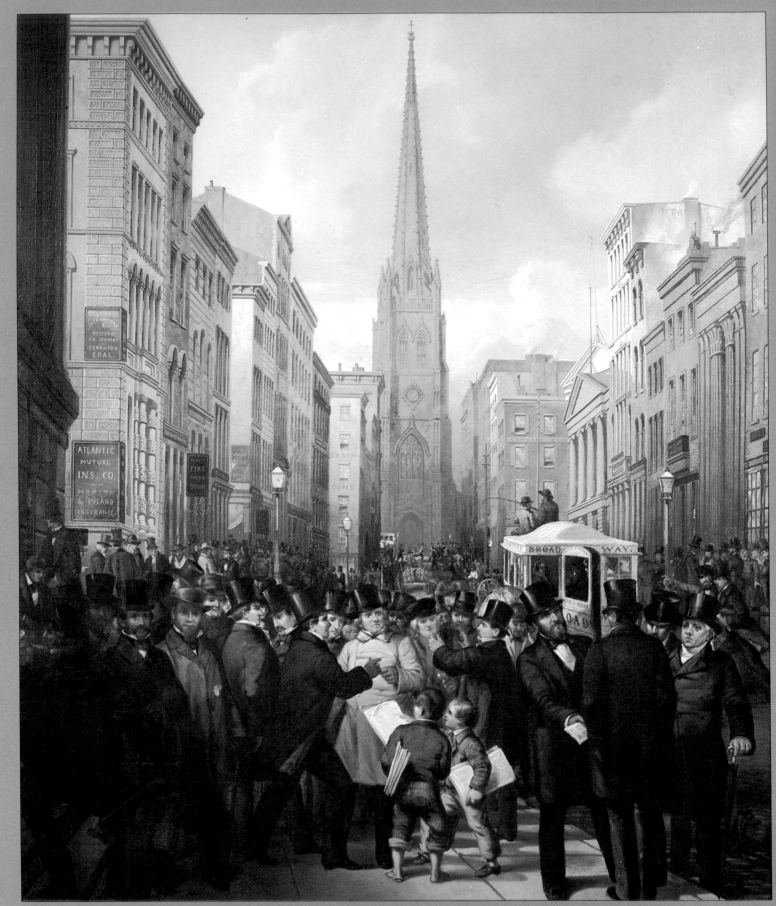

Brokers and speculators thronged Wall Street daily during the War, just as they had during the 1857 banking panic shown in this painting.

Golden Opportunities on Wall Street

As the Union's industries and railroads boomed, so did the value of their stocks. Speculation ran rampant, and Wall Street became an El Dorado for opportunists.

The mania to buy and sell drew crowds that overflowed the staid halls of the Stock Exchange. Every day thousands of shares changed hands on the sidewalks of Wall Street and at nearby hotels and restaurants.

The most frenzied speculation was in gold, the specie always most valued as a hedge against hard times. Rumors of peace, or word of a Northern victory, brought the price of gold down; Northern defeats sent the price soaring, and those traders who had gambled against the Union jubilantly sang "Dixie" in the gold exchange (right).

Fortunes were made, lost and made again on Wall Street, sometimes overnight. New York had three millionaires when the War began, and hundreds when it ended.

Speculators bid feverishly in the Gold Room, the gold exchange's new headquarters, which opened in 1864. The price of a year's membership in the exchange jumped from $200 to $2,500 during the War.

The marble-columned Custom House, headquarters for the collection of import tariffs, dominates the intersection of Wall and Broad Streets. Beginning in 1863, this imposing structure also housed a branch of the U.S. Treasury, and the building's vaults held much of the government's gold supply.

Living in Luxury on Wartime Profits

For a fortunate minority of New Yorkers, the privations of war did not exist. The members of this select new society were making money fast in war-related enterprises — and spending it even faster.

Such New Yorkers built multistoried homes on Fifth Avenue equipped with steam heat, gas lighting and indoor plumbing. They filled these mansions with ornate furniture, patterned carpets and works of art, imported in quantity from abroad.

The new rich in New York were not reticent about displaying their war-begotten wealth. They entertained lavishly and dashed about town in shining carriages. Fashions for women dictated a different costume for every activity. Formal gowns were colorful concoctions of ruffles and bows built around great hoop skirts. The men were also splendidly attired, sporting top hats, lace-trimmed shirts and diamond buttons that sparkled from their waistcoats.

A young woman plays the piano in the ornately furnished parlor of an upper-class Brooklyn home in 1865.

"Heaven save the ladies, how they dress!" exclaimed Charles Dickens on a prewar visit to New York. The women below, pictured in *Godey's Lady's Book* in 1862, wore gowns of silk and satin underpinned by a large hoop.

GODEY'S FASHIONS FOR FEBRUARY 1862.

th Avenue in 1865, seen in a view uptown from 28th Street, was a serenely shaded thoroughfare of wide sidewalks, churches and newly constructed mansions.

A Life of Squalor for the Immigrant Poor

A shipload of Irish immigrants lands at New York's Battery for processing at Castle Garden (*left*). The trunk at right is crudely labeled "Pat Murfy for Ameriky."

Between New York's finest avenues, the city's immigrant masses lived in squalid tenements and shantytowns. For them, the War only made hard times worse. Price-gouging merchants squeezed the slum dwellers without restraint, and the so-called "plunder-mongers" of City Hall did little to help the poor — except to buy their votes on Election Day. The Five Points slum district (*right*) was described by a visiting British journalist as a "miserable haunt of vice and misery."

A man could escape the slums by joining the Army for $13 a month, and by 1863 eighty thousand New Yorkers had done so, confirming the complaint that it was "a rich man's war fought with poor man's blood."

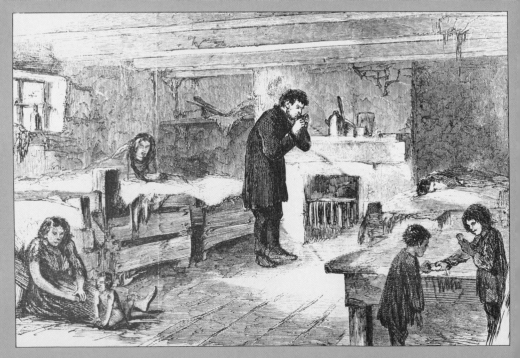

A woodcut of an immigrant family in a squalid East Side shanty illustrated a New York magazine story on the city's bitter poverty in 1860.

Ragged children stand for a photograph in a lane that served as both roadway and sewer in the Five Points — where, it was said, a murder occurred every night.

52

A Showplace for Music and Melodrama

New Yorkers of every social rank loved a good show, and the War only increased their ardor for amusements.

Like so much else in New York, most of the entertainment was imported. Italian opera found its first permanent American home at the Academy of Music (below), where a choice tier of 15 boxes was the domain of the city's leading families. Such American-born actors as Edwin Forrest and Edwin Booth shared New York's thriving stages with the best performers from Europe.

The bombastic showman Phineas T. Barnum scoured the world — or claimed he did — for attractions to fill his five-story American Museum in New York. Few visitors with a quarter to spend could resist gaping at his imported menagerie of lions, tigers and other wild beasts, or gawking at his exotic Fiji cannibals, Circassian maidens and Siamese twins. Barnum's greatest attraction, the two-foot-tall Tom Thumb, whose wedding was the social event of 1863, was billed as an import from England, though he was born in Connecticut.

Barnum aimed his exhibitions at the common man's purse, yet even he was forced to go along with wartime inflation. In 1863 he raised the museum's admission price from 25 to 35 cents.

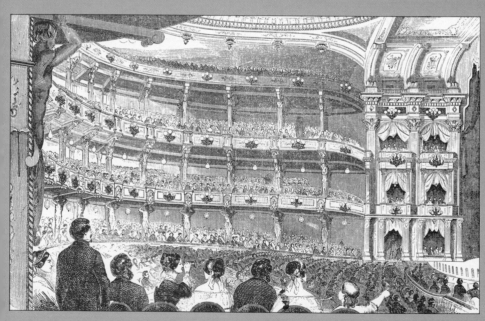

Elegant patrons of grand opera thronged to the Academy of Music on 14th Street, which boasted an immense stage and tiered seating for 4,600.

P. T. Barnum's American Museum on Broadway attracted thousands of visitors each day to a wondrous display of wild animals and human curios, including the world's best-known midget, Tom Thumb, and his wife, Lavinia (inset).

An 1863 handbill for Niblo's Garden advertises the appearance of American tragedian Edwin Forrest as King Lear. So popular was Forrest that a riot once ensued when a visiting British actor challenged the American's dominance of the New York stage.

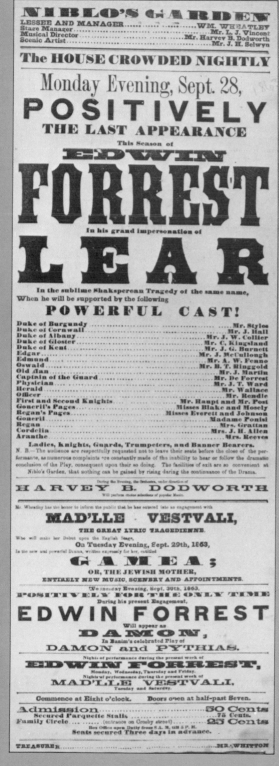

Ice skaters skim across a frozen lake in Central Park, which opened formally in 1864. The wooden shanties on the slope at rear mark the southern edge of the park, at about 59th Street.

The Enterprising Union

"It may well surprise ourselves and all other nations that, during a year of the greatest civil war on record, our country has been wonderfully prosperous."

SCIENTIFIC AMERICAN, JANUARY 17, 1863

A favorite vision of Southern editorial writers in the early months of the Civil War was of grass sprouting up in the streets of New York City. The withdrawal of Southern trade from Yankee markets, these writers proclaimed, would soon bring economic ruin to the enemy's largest city — and by implication to the whole of the North.

One traveler from the South was quoted as having actually seen grass thrusting through the pavement of a once-busy New York thoroughfare. The Richmond *Daily Examiner* printed eyewitness accounts of New York's "silent streets" and "deserted hotels." The "glory of the once-proud metropolis is gone," concluded the *Daily Examiner,* "for the trade of the South will never return."

However partisan that view, it seemed for a while to have some basis in fact. At the outbreak of war, the South owed $300 million to Northern merchants — a debt that the North would have to write off almost totally. That loss, together with the disappearance of Southern customers, the collapse of banks that depended on the cotton trade, the closing of the Mississippi River to commercial traffic — and the perverse uncertainty of the War itself — plunged the North into a financial crisis almost as soon as the guns started firing. To some, it looked as though the North would lose the War by financial default.

Yet the worst never quite happened: By mid-1862 the crisis was over, and by 1863 the Union was well launched on a boom that would last through the War and beyond. The reasons for this remarkable recovery were many and diverse. But they all stemmed from the vast industrial and agricultural potential of the Union's states and territories — a reserve that proved rich beyond almost anyone's imagining.

This extraordinary potential was by no means evident when Salmon Portland Chase took office as Lincoln's Secretary of the Treasury in March 1861. A strait-laced former Ohio governor and senator, Chase was a political appointee with no past financial experience. He found himself saddled from the start with a Treasury that was spending more than it was taking in, and one with rigidly limited revenue sources.

The Treasury got most of its money from customs and the sale of public lands. Neither source could be expanded quickly enough to meet the government's needs. Chase figured he would need $320 million through June of 1862. Counting on a short war, he made the unfortunate decision to raise only $80 million by taxation and attempt to amass the rest by the sale of bonds and Treasury notes. The federal offering was poorly received by a public uncertain about the future of the nation. And the War, Chase soon realized, was going to be far more expensive than he or anyone else had thought; by the fall of 1861 there were already twice as many men in uniform as he had anticipated.

In a dark and cavernous foundry across the Hudson River from West Point, ironworkers direct a stream of molten metal into a cannon mold set in a deep pit. The Union Army's urgent need for ordnance helped generate unprecedented industrial growth in the North.

The state of the nation's business was terrible. "Never before perhaps in the history of this country," wrote the New York *Tribune,* "has such a feeling of uncertainty, of alternate hope and fear, prevailed in the business community." With confidence down and prices depressed, nearly 6,000 businesses failed in 1861.

The blow fell most heavily on Midwestern farmers and merchants who had dealt regularly with Southern buyers. Corn prices dipped so low that some farmers chose to burn their corn as fuel rather than sell it. The price of hogs declined by half. In hard-hit Cincinnati, furniture manufacturers shipped only a third as many pieces during the first five months of the War as they had during the same period a year earlier. Iron production in the Union dropped by 14 per cent, coal production was off, and two of the nation's leading industries, cotton textiles and shoes, suffered precipitous declines. In time, many of these industries would recoup their losses and prosper through Army contracts and other war-generated business. But in the first year of the conflict, the loss of Southern markets was calamitous.

The financial crisis worsened in the week between Christmas of 1861 and New Year's. The supply of gold and silver coins was dwindling rapidly. The federal government was required by law to pay its debts in specie, and was making enormous payments of gold and silver coins to war contractors. In addition, private citizens were hoarding vast amounts of specie. Eyeing the depletion of their reserves, bankers in New York, Philadelphia and Boston suspended all payments in coin on December 30. This meant that the various paper currencies commonly issued by banks throughout the country could no longer be redeemed in specie. If the situation continued, a crippling deflation of those notes would surely result.

The beleaguered Chase and a worried Congress recognized that urgent action was now essential. They needed a dependable currency to enable the government to pay its bills and remain solvent, and they needed more money in circulation to increase purchasing power and thus help businesses to rebound.

Congressman Elbridge Spaulding of New York, formerly a banker in Buffalo, proposed that the government issue its own currency unbacked by gold or silver. The so-called "greenback" notes would be legal tender and thus could be used to pay debts. Spaulding's plan, as his critics immediately pointed out, was unprecedented, risky and perhaps unconstitutional: Only specie had been accepted as legal tender before this. Those opposed argued that increased taxes and the sale of government bonds offered a safer, less inflationary method of raising money and that the issuance of unsupported paper money amounted to a confession of bankruptcy. Once that deceptively easy strategy was embraced, Senator Justin Smith Morrill of Vermont protested, "the doors of the temple of paper money would not soon again be closed." To some, it seemed that greenbacks were practically immoral. A banker declared that gold and silver were the only true measures of value, hav-

ing been "prepared by the Almighty for this very purpose."

Chase himself harbored misgivings about setting the government printing presses in motion. Long a champion of "hard money," he was loath to accept paper as legal tender. Yet Spaulding contended that these were "extraordinary times, and extraordinary measures must be resorted to." Reluctantly, Chase concurred. "The Treasury is nearly empty," he informed Congress early in 1862.

Congress responded in February by passing the first in a series of legal-tender acts that would authorize the printing of $450 million in currency during the War. These greenbacks would be acceptable in all trans-

Treasury Secretary Salmon P. Chase first gained notice in his native Ohio as a lawyer and zealous abolitionist. His Cincinnati law office defended so many fugitive slaves that Chase was grudgingly known in slaveholding Kentucky as "the attorney general for runaway Negroes."

actions save two—the collection of import duties and the payment of the interest due on government bonds.

The chief danger inherent in printing greenbacks was the impetus they would give to inflation. Prices began to climb almost immediately after the first issue and continued to rise throughout the War, with wage increases trailing behind. Many wage earners were thus left with less purchasing power than they had enjoyed before the War. And partly because the government had to pay inflated prices for war materials, the national debt rose to levels previously unthinkable.

Still, inflation in the North never approached the ruinous levels experienced in the South. One important reason was that Congress complemented the legal-tender acts with tax legislation that soaked up a great deal of inflationary currency. In August 1861, Congress had approved the first income tax ever levied by the United States government: Individuals were taxed at a rate of 3 per cent on all income over $800. Then on July 1, 1862, an internal-revenue law was enacted that taxed virtually everything else. There were excise taxes on all luxuries—tobacco, liquor, yachts, billiard tables, gold and silver plate. There were also license taxes, legal-document taxes, inheritance taxes and value-added taxes. Someone calculated that the manufacture and sale of a carriage yielded the government revenue in four ways: First, the leather, cloth, wood and metal were taxed as raw materials; then the manufacturer was taxed for assembling the parts and the dealer for selling the finished product; finally, the purchaser was charged the excise tax levied on luxury items.

The practitioners of every trade, business and profession—from banking and medicine to horse-trading and street-juggling—had to pay a license tax in order to pursue their occupations. Butchers paid the government 5 cents for every sheep they slaughtered, 10 cents for every hog and 30 cents for every steer.

The Union raised 21 per cent of its revenues through taxes during the War, and 13 per cent by printing paper money. By contrast, the Confederacy raised less than 5 per cent by taxes and 60 per cent of its funds by issuing paper money. The result was that while the Confederacy suffered more than 9,000 per cent inflation over the course of the War, inflation in the North was held to a tolerable 80 per cent.

The free-flowing greenbacks gave the economy the infusion of capital and credit it so desperately needed. Buoyed by immediate public acceptance, the notes, in the words of a writer for *Harper's*, "circulated like the fertilizing dew." They enabled manufacturers to expand, kept cash registers ringing in the stores and gave farmers the wherewithal to pay off loans. Commenting on the upswing, *Scientific American* marveled extravagantly that "want has been unfelt in the land."

Of course, the greenbacks alone did not account for the full measure of the Union's wartime prosperity. Military contracts, the extraordinary productivity of both the land and the people, Yankee adaptability and inventiveness, the discovery of new riches in the earth—all of these contributed to the dramatic turnaround. And the boom, in turn, touched off changes in the American economic structure that would survive the War.

A Riot of Currencies

In addition to money issued by the government, a dazzling array of privately coined and printed currency circulated in the Union during the Civil War. Hundreds of state and city banks issued notes, and Northern merchants created their own currencies when wartime hoarding of copper coins led to an acute shortage of small change. Many merchants had scrip printed for their stores, and 8,000 places of business also minted tokens.

Even postage stamps were employed as substitutes for scarce coins. To protect the fragile stamps, a number of merchants enclosed them in small brass and mica cases, designed for the purpose by an enterprising inventor. The cases were embossed with the name of the store that issued them.

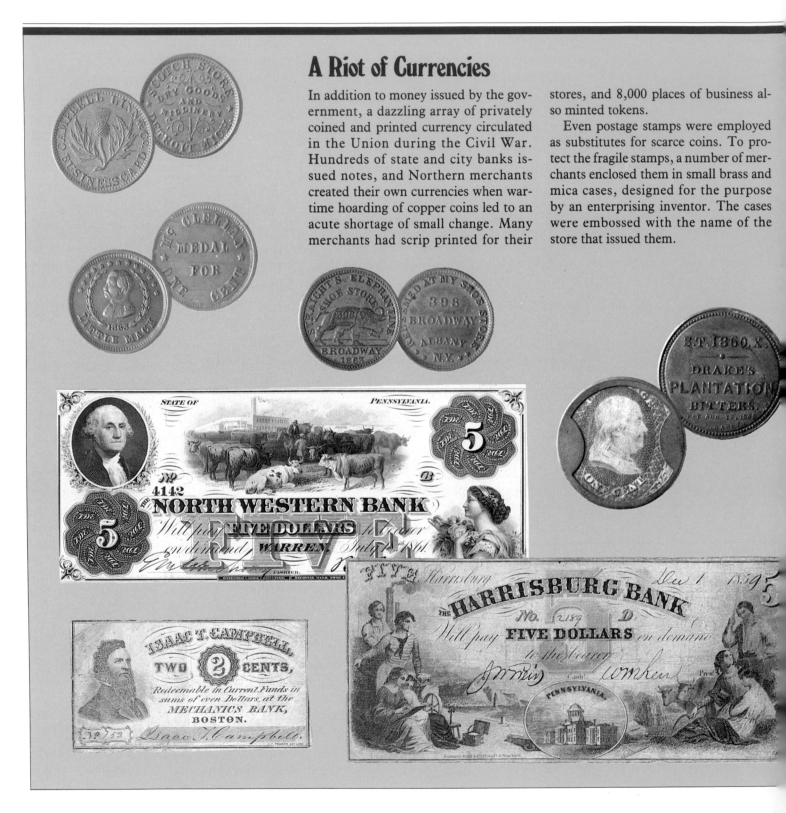

A farmer uses a horse-drawn mower to cut his hay. As field hands went off to war, farmers relied more and more on labor-saving devices; sales of mowers increased tenfold in the first two years of the War.

Driving a horse rake, a farmer gathers cut hay. The rake, like many other innovations in agricultural machinery, had been invented prior to the War, but only wartime necessity persuaded farmers to give up traditional tools.

Among the chief beneficiaries of the wartime prosperity were those who worked the land — although nothing appeared more unlikely at the start of the War. On the farms, a shortage of manpower seemed inevitable. Fully a third of all Northern farmers trooped off to war — and tens of thousands more departed to try their luck in the mines to the west. From the outbreak of war until the end of 1864, a total of 197,000 men from Illinois joined the Army, along with 70,000 from Iowa, and 75,000 from Wisconsin. "In common with all our frontier towns," wrote a home missionary at a Wisconsin settlement, "we feel the sad effects of the war. From this town of 250 voters 111 have volunteered."

Yet in time several factors served to compensate for the loss of manpower. In fact, most farm states actually recorded population growth during the war years. Some of this increase resulted from natural growth, and some of it from foreign immigration. Illinois received 45,000 wartime immigrants; Wisconsin, 23,000; Iowa, 7,000; Minnesota, 5,000. In addition, uncounted numbers of refugees from the embattled border and slave states fled to the rural North and swelled the farm population.

Then, too, women and children assumed many farm responsibilities. "Just take your gun and go," went a contemporary song, "for Ruth can drive the oxen, John, and I can use the hoe." Tens of thousands of women did just that. A churchman in Kansas wrote of seeing one of the women of his parish toiling in the fields. "Her husband is at Vicksburg," he noted. "With what help she can secure and the assistance of her little children, she is carrying on the farm." An Iowa woman reported that "our hired man left to enlist just as corn planting commenced, so I shouldered my hoe and have worked out ever since." And she added dryly: "I guess my services are just as acceptable as his."

Greatly aiding farm production were the introduction of commercial fertilizers and the rapid adoption of labor-saving equipment. Machines like mowers, reapers, cultivators and planters were revolutionizing

farming. Horsepower began to replace manpower for the heavy work, with a great increase in efficiency: A farmer with a scythe could cut about one acre of hay a day; with a horse-drawn mowing machine he could cut 10 times as much. An Illinois clergyman wrote of seeing "a stout matron riding leisurely upon her cutter" while mowing seven acres of hay in a day.

The production of mowers and reapers tripled during the Civil War to meet the increased demand from farmers. So popular did reapers become that they were sold to large-scale operators by the dozens. One awed observer recalled seeing 146 reapers moving in stately unison across the Illinois prairie.

Acclaiming the agricultural bonanza, the Cincinnati *Gazette* asked rhetorically in 1862 how Ohio could sustain the loss of "a hundred thousand agricultural laborers." By the imaginative use of "labor-saving machinery," the *Gazette* responded. The overall effect of mechanization, proclaimed *Scientific American* in 1863, was to make farming "comparatively child's play to what it was 20 years ago."

The Northern states had more acreage under cultivation during the War than ever before. The passage of the Homestead Act in 1862, after 40 years of Congressional bickering, permitted a farmer to gain title to 160 acres of public land by working it for five years. He needed only be a U.S. citizen, or make plans to become one. By the end of the War, more than 2.5 million acres of prairie and plain had been homesteaded, resulting in a total of nearly 15,000 new farms in Minnesota, Wisconsin, Iowa, Kansas and Nebraska.

On farms old and new the states of the Union grew more wheat in 1862, and again in 1863, than the entire country had produced in the previous record year of 1859. In the space of one year — from 1863 to 1864 — the value of staple crops soared from $955 million to $1.44 billion. So plentiful were harvests that the farms of the Midwest and the East managed to feed the Union's troops and civilians and still have enough left over to double exports to Europe in exchange for gold.

The mechanical capacity to process and store farm products increased with the yields. Chicago doubled its meat-packing facilities by constructing 25 new packing houses in a single year. And the grain elevators hard by the Great Lakes dazzled all who saw them. One impressed observer was the English novelist Anthony Trollope, who toured the North in 1862. Gazing at the endless rivers of wheat pouring from Great Lakes freighters into the grain elevators at Buffalo, he saluted a nation ready "to burst with its own fruits, and be smothered by its own riches."

To travel by rail across the rich plains of the American heartland was an exhilarating experience. The New York *Times* noted in 1864 that the Illinois Central Railroad, built across the prairie just 10 years earlier, now traversed a "boundless cultivated field." To many Americans, the gleaming tracks of the railroads themselves were symbolic of growth. Indeed, the doings of the railroads so intrigued the public that they were covered by the press almost daily. The progress of a new road, the completion of a bridge or tunnel—all of these competed for space with war news.

In terms of mileage, the railroads did not expand much during the war years. While an average of 2,000 miles of track had been laid annually in the previous decade, the average yearly figure from 1862 through 1865 was only about 800 miles. A scarcity of labor and materials and the inflated cost of construction contributed to the inactivity.

On the other hand, the railroads did far more business than they had ever done before. Having built to excess in the 1850s, they suddenly found themselves with more wartime traffic than they could possibly handle. In January 1862, Congress gave President Lincoln the authority to commandeer the railroads for wartime exigencies; he rarely had to, but his mandate guaranteed their cooperation. The trains not only carried the

A westward-bound wagon train stops for supplies in Manhattan, Kansas. In 1862, the U.S. government opened 135 million acres of public land to homesteaders; those working their claims for five years were granted the land free.

Army's troops and matériel, but also hauled freight on an unprecedented scale: The European demand for Midwestern foodstuffs, combined with the Mississippi River blockade, resulted in a flow of freight traffic that strained the rolling stock to its limits. During the War, some roads doubled their volume of traffic.

Three of the four great east-west trunk lines in the North — the Erie, the New York Central and the Pennsylvania — made unprecedented profits. Only the Baltimore & Ohio, which was so close to the front lines that it was frequently disrupted by the fighting, failed to benefit fully from the War. In three years a share of Erie stock rose more than a hundred points, from 17 to 126½, while the Pennsylvania's annual earnings soared from five million dollars in 1860 to $17 million in 1865. The stock of 16 railroads of varying sizes more than doubled in market value — from $70 million in 1862 to $150 million in 1864.

One major expansion of the rail system was completed during the War. The Atlantic & Great Western, built between 1860 and 1864, ran from Salamanca in western New York to Dayton, Ohio. Connections at either end enabled the line to provide through service for the first time from New York City to St. Louis, via Cleveland and Cincinnati. Construction advanced at the rate of a mile a day through New York State, northwestern Pennsylvania and Ohio. Two months after the final piece of track was pounded into place at Dayton in June of 1864, a trainload of invited guests inaugurated the new line by highballing from New York to St. Louis in 44 hours. It was the longest unbroken journey — more than 1,000 miles — then possible in America.

The accelerated use of the railroads led eventually to the adoption of a common-gauge track, a move that greatly facilitated long-distance travel. At the outbreak of war there were at least eight different gauges in use in the North, ranging from four feet eight and a half inches to six feet. This necessitated frequent train changes and aggravating delays. Trains from New York could go direct to Buffalo, for instance, but could not continue by the lake-shore route to Chicago because local railways with five different gauges intervened. In 1864, when work began on the first transcontinental railroad, the narrowest gauge — in use throughout New York and New England — was adopted as the standard.

The railroads, and their patrons, paid a price for the boom in business. Tracks, bridges and rolling stock wore out far faster than they could be replaced — with the result, observed the New York *Sun* in March of 1865, that the headline "Awful Railroad Disaster" had become standard in the daily press. The *Sun* went on to recite a litany of collisions and derailments in which 400 passengers had been killed or injured in a little over two months. "We could name half a dozen railroads," added the *Sun*, "upon which a man has less chance for life and limb in a fifty-mile trip than our soldiers had in the battles of the Wilderness." The prevalence of old engines and rickety cars, the *Sun* asserted, was evidence that "the railroad companies have been in too great a hurry to grow rich."

Even railroad executives acknowledged that the wartime trains were not all that they should be. But the public continued to ride the railroads, and the optimism of the lines' owners remained high. The era, noted the *American Railroad Journal* in 1864, was "the most prosperous ever known to American railways."

That optimism, which was a kind of natural resource in itself, animated almost the whole of the Northern business community. The War imposed restrictions, but it also afforded fantastic opportunities to entrepreneurs shrewd enough to seize them. James Mowry, for example, had been a cotton-goods manufacturer in Norwich, Connecticut, before the War. When secession cut off his supply of raw cotton, he boldly sought and won a government contract to produce 30,000 muskets. Arms-making was a sophisticated process that demanded both skilled labor and intricate machine tools, but Mowry was able to subcontract the making of various parts to local machine shops while he swiftly auctioned off his looms. He managed to transform his textile mill into an arms assembly plant, and within a year he was in full production and on his way to an output of 1,200 muskets a week.

Hundreds of other manufacturers, many of them in New England, performed similar if less spectacular feats to meet wartime needs. An ax producer, switching smoothly to sabers, turned out 7,500 weapons in less than a month; a carriage maker in Walcottville, Connecticut, produced 28 wagons for the Army in 15 days.

One measure of the surge in manufacturing was the increase in factories. In Philadelphia, a leading industrial center, 58 new plants rose in 1862 alone, 57 more in 1863 and 63 in 1864. Six new factories opened in the modest-sized city of New Haven, Connecticut, in a single year.

In some industries, the demands of war prompted manufacturers to embrace innovations that soon generated remarkable growth. The shoe industry, for example, was on the verge of a technological revolution when the War began: A New Englander by the name of Lyman Blake had just invented a shoe-stitching machine that promised to transform the production of shoes from a handcraft to a mass industry. The need to supply thousands of troops in short order helped Blake's invention win swift acceptance, and shoe production quickly doubled. Blake unwisely sold his patent, and before the War was over, the owner of it was collecting $750,000 a year in royalties. A worker in a shoe factory could now turn out several hundred pairs a day, and new factories proliferated. "Operatives are pouring in as fast as room can be made for them," reported a newspaper in Lynn, Massachusetts, then the center of the shoe industry. "The hum of machinery is heard on every hand."

Similarly, the clothing industry benefited enormously from the boost given new technology by the War. The sewing machine, invented by Elias Howe, had come into use in the 1850s. But its commercial possibilities were not fully realized until the Union Army, desperate for uniforms, conceived a set of standard sizes for soldiers and began sending orders to clothing manufacturers. As the practice of making standardized outfits caught on, the mass, ready-made clothing industry was born. The number of sewing machines almost doubled between 1860 and 1865. Clothing manufacture became a mammoth industry.

Woolen mills, galvanized into activity by the disappearance of Southern cotton, enjoyed a boom under the stimulus of contracts for uniforms. Wool production more than doubled, and a number of wool manufacturers amassed profits so stupendous that they were able to reward their stockholders with annual dividends of between 10 and 40 per cent.

Paper manufacturers also enjoyed a heyday, despite the scarcity and expense of cotton rag, the main ingredient of paper before the War. The manufacturers turned to substitutes like straw, wood pulp and corn husks, and garnered enormous profits. Other notably profitable industries included those that produced lumber, alcoholic beverages, farm machinery and minerals of all descriptions. But the Union's most unexpected source of new wealth came from northwestern Pennsylvania, along the banks of a small tributary to the Allegheny River known as Oil Creek.

People had known of petroleum for a long time. The Indians who inhabited the rugged woodlands of western Pennsylvania had observed the dark, foul-smelling liquid collecting in springs and pools and had used it as a liniment. But the Yankee entrepreneurs who began investigating it in the 1850s found that petroleum could also be used both as fuel for lamps and as a lubricant for machine parts. If they could acquire it in quantity, they reasoned, they might have a marketable substitute for whale oil, tallow and vegetable fats. In the summer of 1859, a 38-year-old former railroad conductor named Edwin Drake erected a wooden derrick along Oil Creek and began drilling. Sixty-nine feet down he struck oil, and he was soon pumping it at the rate of 20 barrels a day.

The news of Drake's discovery precipi-

Women assemble cartridges for Union rifles in a Watertown, Massachusetts, arsenal. It was dangerous work: Explosions in two arsenals in 1864 killed a total of 41 women.

The Connecticut Yankee Who Armed the Union

In February 1861, seeing war clouds on the horizon, a Connecticut arms maker wired his factory superintendent: "Run the armory night and day with double sets of hands — I had rather have an accumulation of our arms than to have money lying idle."

The author of this urgent dispatch, Samuel Colt, inventor of the revolver, was well prepared when the fighting broke out. Between 1861 and 1865, his sprawling Hartford factory, despite a devastating fire, turned out an enormous number of weapons for the Northern forces. The War Department purchased 146,840 of the enterprising Yankee's revolvers — more than 40 per cent of the total bought by the federal government during the conflict. Colt's company also produced a revolving rifle, which it sold to state militias, and from 1862 on, a single-shot rifle, which saw service in the U.S. Army.

Samuel Colt's factory, built in 1854, was the world's largest private armory, employing more than 1,500 workmen. It had 160,000 square feet of floor space and housed a steam power plant with a 30-foot flywheel.

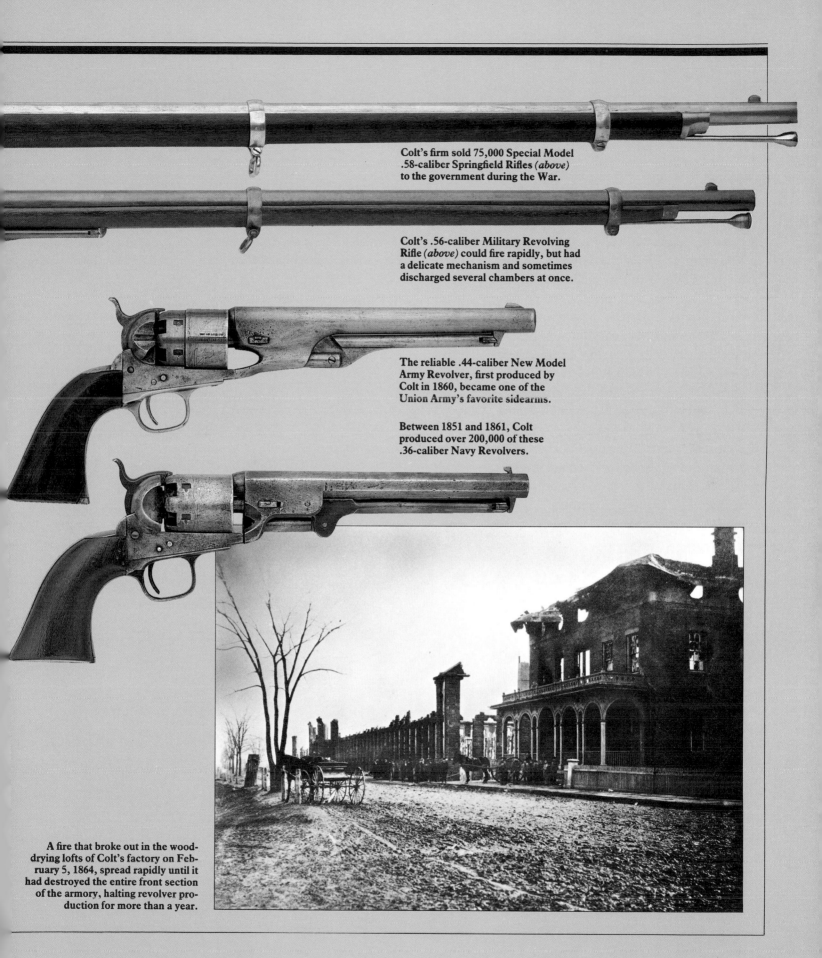

Colt's firm sold 75,000 Special Model .58-caliber Springfield Rifles (*above*) to the government during the War.

Colt's .56-caliber Military Revolving Rifle (*above*) could fire rapidly, but had a delicate mechanism and sometimes discharged several chambers at once.

The reliable .44-caliber New Model Army Revolver, first produced by Colt in 1860, became one of the Union Army's favorite sidearms.

Between 1851 and 1861, Colt produced over 200,000 of these .36-caliber Navy Revolvers.

A fire that broke out in the wood-drying lofts of Colt's factory on February 5, 1864, spread rapidly until it had destroyed the entire front section of the armory, halting revolver production for more than a year.

tated a stampede to the sleepy lowlands along Oil Creek, where prospectors began buying or leasing land from local farmers. In quest of worthwhile drilling sites, newcomers roamed the area holding Y-shaped "divining rods." Others sought guidance from their dreams, while some tried literally to sniff out the substance; in time, men with allegedly unique olfactory gifts appeared on the scene to offer prospectors their services as "oil smellers."

Through 1860 and 1861 the gushers continued to burst from the banks of Oil Creek. One well, known as "the Fountain," spewed oil 10 feet in the air and yielded 10 barrels an hour; another poured forth an astonishing 2,500 barrels a day for several months. Soon there were 74 producing wells on Oil Creek. The New York *Herald* proclaimed "the new gospel of Saint Petroleum."

Overproduction depressed the market temporarily, but by the end of 1862 prices were climbing toward new heights. Profits were astronomical: One well owner earned more than $2.5 million in 15 months. Others squandered fortunes as fast as they made them. Part of the rapidly growing legend of the oil fields concerned "Coal Oil Johnny" Steele, who happened to inherit a farm sitting atop a large reservoir of oil. With his royalty income of $2,000 a day he hired a minstrel troupe and a private train, and amused himself by traveling about the country putting on shows wherever the fancy took him. When he had blown his whole fortune, he took a job as a baggage agent on the Oil Creek Railroad.

But more durable fortunes were also born in the oil fields. Among them was that acquired by a diminutive young Scotsman named Andrew Carnegie, who had emigrat-

ed to America in 1848 at the age of 12. Carnegie worked as a bobbin boy in a textile factory and as a telegraph operator before getting a low-paying job as a superintendent with the Pennsylvania Railroad. In 1861, he took a chance and invested in the nascent Columbia Oil Company. Carnegie continued to work for the railroad and in time helped to

Edwin Drake, in top hat, stands with a friend by the first commercially productive oil well in the United States, completed by Drake in 1859 near Titusville, Pennsylvania. Others grew rich from his discovery that oil could be pumped from between layers of rock, but Drake sold out early and was broke within 10 years.

organize the military telegraph (he never enlisted, however, choosing instead to purchase a substitute). His firm, meanwhile, pumped 2,000 barrels a day and in a single year paid out more than a million dollars on an investment of $40,000. Impatient for an even better return, Carnegie multiplied his earnings many times by investing them in the steel industry on the eve of its spectacular growth.

Equally astute was 23-year-old John D. Rockefeller, who realized that what the oil business lacked was a major refinery not too far from the fields themselves and with good rail and water connections to the East. He picked Cleveland as the ideal site and in 1863, with four partners, built a refinery near the Cuyahoga River. Subsequently, Rockefeller bought out all his partners but one and launched the ambitious program of expansion and consolidation that eventually gave him control of the oil industry. Like young Carnegie, he avoided military service by buying a substitute.

So rapid was the growth of the petroleum industry that by war's end oil was the North's sixth largest export. "It is difficult," said the English banker S. Morton Peto, "to find a parallel to such a blessing bestowed upon a nation in the hour of her direst necessity."

At about the same time that Edwin Drake made his strike on Oil Creek, great gold and silver deposits were discovered in the Comstock Lode in the Nevada Territory. Thus began a gold-and-silver rush to Nevada, and to the other potentially rich territories of Colorado, Idaho and Montana. The Comstock Lode, near Virginia City — which overnight became the second largest town west of the Rockies — was producing

$15 million in ore annually, luring honest adventurers along with less savory types, including draft dodgers, deserters and swindlers of all descriptions.

Caravans made up of as many as 1,200 wagons raised great clouds of dust on the routes west. "Day after day," wrote the Reverend Jonathan Blanchard, on his way to Idaho, "they trudge on, with sand in their eyes, sand in their ears, sand in their hair, neck, bosom, boots, stockings, hats, clothing, victuals, drink, bed clothes; their bed is sand." As for the motive animating them, he concluded, it was simple greed — "the one all-absorbing master passion of the whole region."

Most of those who lusted after quick wealth were grievously disappointed, but there were enough spectacular successes to keep the multitudes coming. The Comstock Lode yielded $300 million in 20 years, the Gregory Lode in the Colorado Territory about $22 million in five years, and lesser lodes in the Idaho and Montana Territories about $14 million in three years.

An atmosphere of lawlessness and violence pervaded the mining towns. The saloons and muddy thoroughfares of another Virginia City, this one in Montana, swarmed with murderous gangs whose members had little reason to fear arrest. When some semblance of order was brought to the community in 1864, it was imposed by a vigilance committee of citizens rather than by law officers. "In the first three days of the acts of this committee," reported the *Boston Review,* "forty persons were arrested, tried, condemned and executed, among whom were the sheriff and one or two of his deputies, several other county officers, and men of apparently good standing, many of whom con-

A working model of an oil well is hauled down Fifth Avenue during a New York City parade in March 1865. A sign on the float proclaims: "Oil Is King Now, Not Cotton." By war's end, eager investors had incorporated 1,100 petroleum companies.

fessed their guilt before death. This summary proceeding sent terror to the hearts of all who belonged to the gang, and they fled to parts unknown."

A similar spirit of lawlessness, if not violence, plagued the business community in the East. The old Protestant work ethic, which decried conspicuous consumption and encouraged wordly success only to glorify God, now seemed to be giving way to the pursuit of wealth by any means. "The greatest disadvantage of the war," commented the editor of the New York *Times* in 1863, was "the prosperity of the country." In a sense, he was right. Wealth was breeding corruption: Everything, it seemed, was for sale. Middlemen, or so-called contract brokers, let manufacturers know that lucrative War Department contracts were to be

had if the right individuals were paid off. A Senator from Rhode Island, James F. Simmons, collected $10,000 for his services in securing a contract for a rifle manufacturer.

Representatives for the liquor interests, learning that the government intended to raise the tax on whiskey in 1864, bribed members of Congress not to make the tax applicable to existing stocks. When the new tax regulations went into effect, distilleries immediately raised their prices but paid the old tax rate on stock already on hand. Their profits from that maneuver were estimated at $50 million.

Too often during the war years, the line between the government and private interests all but disappeared. One member of the board of the Onondaga Salt Company in upstate New York, for example, was the speaker of the state legislature in Albany; another director was a member of the Ways and Means Committee in Washington. Through their influence, lobbyists for the company had little difficulty obtaining exclusive rights to the great salt deposits near Syracuse, together with a federal tariff so steep it kept out foreign imports. The Onondaga company then doubled the price of its salt and reaped enormous profits.

The federal government itself was routinely defrauded in its dealings with private contractors and suppliers of all descriptions. In one notorious case that came to the attention of an investigating commission, an agent charged with acquiring vessels for the Navy was suspected of purchasing craft he knew to be unseaworthy and then selling them to the government for twice what he had paid.

Even more audacious was the deal in which a speculator named Arthur Eastman bought from the War Department a large quantity of old but still serviceable rifles at $3.50 apiece. Eastman sold the weapons to another speculator, Simon Stevens, for $12.50 apiece. Incredibly, Stevens then turned around and sold the whole lot back to the Army, charging $22 for each rifle. The triple transaction yielded a total profit exceeding 600 per cent.

But the case that attracted the most attention involved one Alexander Cummings, who became a government purchasing agent through the intervention of his old friend Simon Cameron, Lincoln's first Secretary of War. Cummings proceeded to line the pockets of his friends in business by purchasing from them such nonessential items as straw hats and linen trousers, together with huge quantities of ale, pickles and tongue — all at grossly inflated prices. Secre-tary Cameron was censured by the House of Representatives for tolerating Cummings' activities, but the purchasing agent himself was never charged.

Cameron was also severely reprimanded for granting government favors to his family-controlled Northern Central Railroad at the expense of the competing Baltimore & Ohio. Cameron's dealings at the War Department eventually became so notorious that he was forced to resign.

In 1863, a War Department official was sent to investigate reports of corruption and profiteering in the occupied city of Memphis. The official discovered a vast illicit market in cotton; Federal soldiers were buying it from Southerners and reselling it to eager Northern dealers. "Every colonel, captain, or quartermaster is in secret partnership with some operator in cotton," the official reported. "Every soldier dreams of adding a bale of cotton to his monthly pay." The practice was so common, he concluded, that it had "to an alarming extent corrupted the army."

Indeed, trade with the enemy was perhaps the most demoralizing and widespread of all the shady business that afflicted the wartime economy. Officially forbidden by both the Confederate and Union commands, such traffic was nevertheless inevitable. The two sides had been economically interdependent before the War, and trading between them was a long-established tradition. The South had cotton, and it desperately needed shoes, salt, medicine and munitions. A Northern trader in 1864 could buy cotton for 10 or 20 cents a pound in Memphis or New Orleans and sell it for $1.90 in Boston. Or he could pick up a sack of salt for $1.25 in the North and sell it for $60 in the South.

Workmen at the Jackson Mine in northern Michigan load iron ore into rail carts. With the opening of the Sault Ste. Marie Canal, which linked Lake Superior with the other Great Lakes, this remote region doubled its ore shipments.

Not even "a Chinese wall from the Atlantic to the Pacific," remarked a foreign observer, could have choked off a trade with such potential for profit.

Commenting in 1863 on the immense size of the traffic in the Mississippi River region, General Ulysses S. Grant noted wryly that "no honest man has made money in West Tennessee in the last year"—adding that "many fortunes" had been made there during the same period.

Many of the smuggling schemes along the thousand-mile frontier between North and South showed considerable ingenuity. One woman in Tennessee was stopped while making her way toward Confederate lines in a voluminous skirt; discovered tied to a girdle beneath it were twelve pairs of boots—each stuffed with medicine and whiskey. In Memphis, a funeral attracted the suspicion of authorities; the coffin turned out to be crammed with medicine destined for General Earl Van Dorn's Confederate army to the east.

One of the most brazen traders was the Union's Colonel Andrew J. Butler, who was said to have made a fortune in New Orleans while his brother, General Benjamin Butler, was commander of the occupying forces there. According to the report of an angry Treasury Department official in 1862, Colonel Butler was in Louisiana "for the sole purpose of making money."

In December of 1862, Benjamin Butler was replaced in New Orleans by General Nathaniel Banks—who was immediately offered a bribe of $100,000 to approve a shady deal. A disillusioned Banks wrote his wife that "everybody connected with the government has been employed in stealing." He commented sadly: "I never despaired of my country until I came here.''

Banks was by no means the only one who despaired of what he witnessed in the free-spending wartime years. The New York *Herald* coined a new epithet — "shoddy" — to describe the whole era. Originally, the word referred to a flimsy material used by profiteering contractors to make Army uniforms that were so poor they tended to disintegrate in the rain. "The world has seen its iron age, its silver age, its golden age and its brazen age," pronounced the *Herald*. "This is the age of shoddy." It was characterized by "shoddy brokers in Wall Street, or shoddy manufacturers of shoddy goods, or shoddy contractors for shoddy articles." On Sundays, concluded the *Herald*, these men became "shoddy Christians."

Some of the upright business interests agreed with the *Herald*. The New York Chamber of Commerce acknowledged in a report that the city had its share of shoddy merchants, some of whom had supplied the government with shoes whose soles were stiffened with pasteboard and wooden shingles. One manufacturer was taken to task for producing a boot whose sole dropped off after a half hour's march. He defended himself by saying that the boot was intended for use by the cavalry.

It was a time, as the *Herald* noted, when profit was everything. "The individual who makes the most money, no matter how," complained the *Herald*, was assumed to be "the greatest man." Eyeing the lucrative deals to be turned, Union General Cadwal-

A caustic wartime cartoon depicts unscrupulous clothing manufacturers selling shoddy goods to government agents, and on the right, the tattered victim of their greed. It was estimated that fully one fifth of the Army's purchases were tainted by corruption.

The Albany Contracters who have "influence" at Washington, and   Their Victim.

lader Washburn wrote wistfully to his brother that "if I could now be at home, I would rake down largely!"

Few raked down as largely as the speculators in securities and gold. Stock prices were acutely sensitive to fluctuations in the fortunes of the Union armies, rising with their victories and falling with reversals. For an astute investor, the situation was made to order. The prospect of a long war, a leading financier was heard to remark after the first Battle of Bull Run, promised a fortune for "every man in Wall Street who is not a natural idiot."

In 1862, stock values increased an average of 40 per cent, while many popular shares rose to triple their prewar price. A financial writer recalled that sometimes the buying fever "amounted almost to insanity." On one day in January 1862, he noted, trading became so chaotic that "the same stock on the same call was often selling at one and two per cent higher at one end of the room than at the other."

A Wall Street observer recalled that day after day the city exchanges were blocked by a mass of speculators "frenzied by the general passion for gain." Included in their number were a sprinkling of daring women — "Crinoline in Wall Street," as the *Herald* referred to the phenomenon.

In 1864 stock sales in New York alone rose from $25 million a day to more than $100 million a day. Those who profited the most were the insiders — politicians and bankers in Washington and New York — who had advance information about military moves and political developments.

Gold speculation was regarded by many as particularly harmful to wartime morale. Only gold would retain intrinsic value as a medium of exchange in the event of economic collapse. Therefore, bad news increased the price of the metal while good news diminished it. Such a profit could be made on Confederate victories that Horace Greeley referred to those who traded in the metal as "Jeff Davis gold gamblers."

On one occasion, two journalists of the Brooklyn *Daily Eagle* managed to inflate the price of gold by circulating a false report of a presidential call for further conscription and a "day of fasting, humiliation and prayer." The moral of this gambit, concluded Greeley's New York *Tribune*, was that on Wall Street, "no lie is so big that it cannot be swallowed."

While many in the financial and business communities were "gainers by the internal troubles that afflict the country," as the Chicago Board of Trade put it, members of the laboring class were experiencing hard times. Indeed, the gap between rich and poor was growing steadily wider. By mid-war, New York could claim several hundred millionaires — including the dry goods merchant Alexander Stewart, who was paying $400,000 in taxes on an annual income of four million dollars. Yet many a New York laborer was scarcely keeping up with the cost of living.

Although inflation remained relatively low, it still outstripped wages. Between 1861 and 1863, while eggs were increasing in price from 15 cents to 25 cents a dozen, potatoes from $1.50 to $2.25 a bushel, and cheese from 8 cents to 18 cents a pound, the average daily wage of a blacksmith was rising only from $1.75 to $2.00, and that of common laborers from $1.00 to $1.25.

Among the most exploited workers were those women who labored as seamstresses.

Employed by both the government and private contractors, seamstresses — who had to supply their own thread — were paid only pennies for making articles of clothing that took several hours to sew. A woman in New York earned 17 cents for making four pairs of drawers in a 14-hour day; the average week's wage for a seamstress was a pathetic $1.54. Women umbrella makers in New York earned six to eight cents for each of the dozen umbrellas they could turn out in an 18-hour workday; in 1863 they went on strike for a two-cent-an-umbrella raise and got it.

The workers — like the rest of the population — were caught up in a period of rapid economic change, and they coped with it as best they could. Stubbornly, they campaigned for higher wages, agitated against the immigration of foreign laborers, and demanded an end to 14-hour shifts in favor of an eight-hour day. Workers in various industries protested the steady march of mechanization, opposing the introduction of new devices that threatened to make thousands of jobs obsolete.

The laborers' path to a better life was frequently blocked, however. Labor unions were assailed as unpatriotic, and strikes were repressed by troops, or defeated by the use of women, free blacks and immigrants as strikebreakers.

Yet the fundamental economic change of the war years lay beyond the workers' growing militancy. When the prominent New York merchant Abiel A. Low looked back after the War and tried to summarize the important changes, he fixed on one above all others — the focusing of economic power in fewer and larger corporations. The war years gave birth to great, often monopo-

listic enterprises that reached beyond regional markets to sell their goods and services on a continental scale. The Western Union Telegraph Company, for example, set out to absorb the 50 local telegraph companies providing regional services. By 1866, Western Union had built or acquired 75,000 miles of line and eliminated all of its rivals.

And throughout the War, the more powerful railroad lines expanded by merger, absorbing scores of smaller roads. The Pennsylvania Railroad, for example, gained control of the line from Harrisburg to Lancaster in 1861 and later added the Philadelphia & Erie. Expanding westward, the Pennsylvania swallowed the Pittsburgh, Fort Wayne & Chicago and captured a significant share of the Western trade.

The trend toward monopoly was also visible in the producers' organizations — such as the National Paper Manufacturers' Association — that appeared during the War and frequently fixed prices for their products. It could be seen as well in the establishment of a national banking system, which unified currency and stabilized banking operations.

Few of the corporate mergers offered the public such obvious benefits, however, and many were greeted with suspicion. Popular fear of monopoly forced the Massachusetts legislature to reject the proposed merger of two railroads — the Boston & Worcester and the Western — that vied for the Boston-to-Albany trade. Opponents of the merger pointed out that the proposed capital of the new road would be a "monstrous" and "unheard-of" $15 million — a sum they warned would give the railroad far too much leverage in the politics of the state. There was similar opposition to the Camden & Amboy Railroad's monopoly of the traffic between New York and Philadelphia — although public protest in that case did not prevent the C & A from finally gobbling up the competition.

Similarly ineffectual was public opposition to the Illinois legislature's granting of a monopoly over Chicago's horse-drawn streetcar business. As the Chicago *Tribune* reported it, a gathering of 2,600 people endorsed an angry resolution condemning "the great railroad swindle and the tide of fraud and corruption which is sweeping over our state and municipal affairs." The Governor of Illinois vetoed the monopoly bill, but it was passed again by the legislature and became law.

Centralization in the telegraph and transportation businesses directly affected the public. But there were other mergers whose effects were more difficult for the public to gauge. Salt-mining interests in Michigan, for instance, traveled to New York to study the take-over techniques of the Onondaga Salt Company at Syracuse, and returned to organize three fourths of Michigan's more than 50 salt works into two powerful companies. Much the same thing took place in the nation's shoe and meat-packing industries and in the manufacture of steam engines.

These burgeoning monopolies tended to be dominated by a new breed of capitalists who emerged during the war years — figures such as Rockefeller and Carnegie, the financier J. P. Morgan, the wagon-making Studebaker brothers and the meat packer Philip Armour. Their names were not well known to the public yet, but they soon would be. Gifted with a broader vision than their predecessors, these men were out to create corporate enterprises of the greatest possible magnitude.

In many ways, they epitomized the buoyant and daring spirit of a region that in the midst of war was only beginning to realize its economic strength. But in another way they were atypical: None of them shared with hundreds of thousands of Northerners of their generation the wrenching and exhilarating prospect of turning from citizens into soldiers.

The Birth of the Oil Industry

"Oil City is worthy of its name. The air reeks with oil. The mud is oily. The rocks perspire oil. The water shines with the rainbow hues of oil." So wrote a visitor to the booming complex of petroleum fields along Oil Creek in northwest Pennsylvania in the mid-1860s. After oil was first tapped near the creek in 1859, fortune hunters poured into the region, tearing up forest and field to erect settlements out of the mud.

On hand to witness this phenomenon was an itinerant photographer named John Mather. Nothing escaped his inquisitive eye — the wells, the tank cars and barges, the hard faces of men and women lured by the dream of riches. He worked so close to the gushers he was sometimes drenched in oil. His thousands of photographs — some of which are shown on these and the following pages — captured scenes from boom towns that had flared into sudden life and would just as suddenly disappear.

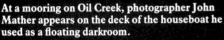

At a mooring on Oil Creek, photographer John Mather appears on the deck of the houseboat he used as a floating darkroom.

Oil derricks stand timber to timber on a field developed near

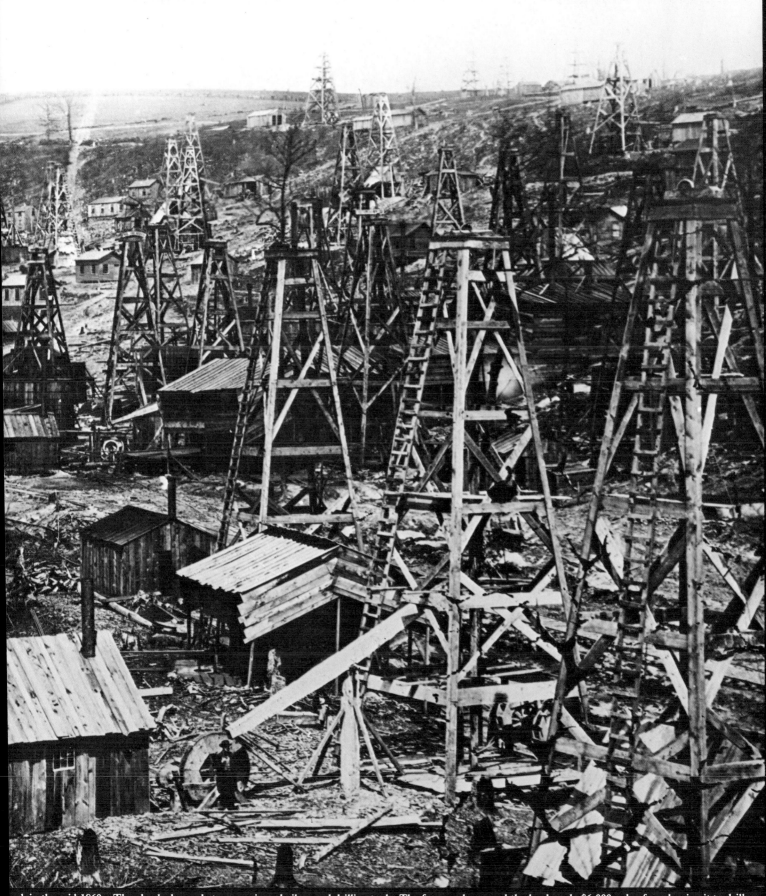

...eek in the mid-1860s. The shacks housed steam engines, boilers and drilling tools. The farmer who owned the land made $6,000 a day from leasing it to drillers.

A wagon loaded with empty drums waits to take on oil from a storage vat. As many as 2,000 wagons a day carried oil from drilling sites to wharves and railheads.

A train carrying barrels of oil leaves the boom town of Rouseville. Traffic was frequently so heavy that loaded cars clogged the tracks around major depots.

Oil flatboats jam the mouth of Oil Creek in 1864. Because the river w

avigable only at high water, boatmen periodically dammed and then unblocked the waterway, floating as many as 250 flatboats downstream on the resulting flood.

Standing amid unpainted shanties, a group of strong-featured Oil Creek matrons gather in their finest fashions for afternoon tea.

In a relaxed moment, oil workers lounge about an engine house and drilling rig around 1864, as a fiddler, guitarist and piper prepare to play.

Mustering the Legions

"This draft will be the experimentum crucis to decide whether we have a government among us."

NEW YORK LAWYER GEORGE TEMPLETON STRONG

"Our village was all alive yesterday with the departure of our braves," wrote the essayist Ralph Waldo Emerson from his home in Concord, Massachusetts. "Judge Hoar made a speech to them at the Depot; Mr. Reynolds made a prayer. And when the whistle of the train was heard, & George Prescott (the commander), who was an image of manly beauty, ordered his men to march, his wife stopped him & put down his sword to kiss him, & grief & pride ruled the hour."

For the citizens of thousands of Northern communities, such emotional scenes at the depot were their first tangible link with the War. Here, for a brief moment, the Northern call to arms ceased to be rhetoric and took on a personal meaning. Almost everybody, it seemed, had a son, brother or friend parading down Main Street and climbing on a train bound for war.

Because the long arm of recruitment touched nearly every Northern community, it stirred unusually widespread and intense feelings. Few issues affected the home front so directly, and few so severely tested the North's resolve to act as a nation.

From the start, the government's approach to mustering an army was tentative and disorganized. Nobody knew for sure whether volunteering would yield enough men, or whether some form of conscription would be necessary. Beyond that, nobody knew how the public would respond to a call to arms, in whatever form it might take. That perceptive student of the American character, Count Alexis de Tocqueville, had written after touring the nation in the 1830s that "the notions and habits of the people of the United States are so opposed to compulsory recruitment that I do not think it can ever be sanctioned by their laws."

Although de Tocqueville was ultimately proved wrong, there were times when it appeared he might be right. The badly flawed conscription law that Congress passed in 1863 did help provide the manpower that the North needed but at a cost that was almost prohibitive. The unfair exemption provisions of the law stirred bitter class resentments and created an entire industry devoted to draft evasion. The draft riots that followed were devastating not only because of their violence (they were the worst civil disorders to have occurred in the United States) but also because of the depth of racial hatred they revealed. They were a grim reminder that a racist mentality was not restricted to the South.

Yet despite all its failings, the draft was generally accepted in the North as a necessary evil, and this acceptance indicated an important change in the American character: In this time of crisis, Americans proved willing to subordinate their own interests — and those of their communities and states — to the demands of the Union. And in acknowledging the Union's authority, people tolerated a greater degree of central direction than ever before in the nation's history. The 1863 draft law, the New York *Times*

This lottery wheel, employed in Wilmington, Delaware, for the military draft in 1864, was built with glass sides so that envelopes containing the names of eligible men could be seen tumbling inside as officials turned the wheel. The envelopes were drawn through the wheel's small trap door.

declared proudly, was the Union's "first assertion of purpose to *command* the means for our preservation."

At the outset, the federal government left the raising of its armies to state and local officials, and to the good will of its citizens. During the War's first year, patriotism alone seemed to be enough to fill the Union ranks. Following the Federal defeat at Bull Run in July 1861, a call for volunteers yielded 91,000 men in only 18 days; by November the Army had already exceeded its authorized strength of 500,000.

In April 1862, after the Federal victories at Fort Henry, Fort Donelson and Shiloh, word went out that no more men were needed. All recruiting offices in the North were closed by order of Secretary of War Edwin Stanton; even the furniture was sold. But it was only a matter of weeks before this decision was recognized as folly and the call for troops was renewed. In early July, with the collapse of General George McClellan's Peninsular Campaign, President Lincoln asked for 300,000 three-year volunteers.

This appeal introduced the state-by-state, population-based quotas that would be used in all subsequent calls for volunteers; the states in turn established quotas for cities and townships. Once again, the recruiting posters went up. "Is There a North?" asked one such poster in Peekskill, New York. The "Live Men" of Peekskill and vicinity were invited to furnish the answer. The war rallies had the flavor of revival meetings, with wounded veterans hobbling on stage like reformed sinners. At a typical meeting in Hartford, Connecticut, revivalist-style speakers studded their exhortations with such phrases as "War! War to the knife! Knife to the

hilt!" — inspiring young men to jump up in a patriotic frenzy and come forward to enlist. When a speaker at another meeting asked for money to encourage enlistments, $20,000 was pledged in five minutes. John S. Gibbons, an editor for the New York *Evening Post*, caught the warlike spirit of the time in a poem that was soon set to music: "We are coming, Father Abraham, three hundred thousand more, / From Mississippi's winding stream and from New England's shore; / We leave our ploughs and workshops, our wives and children dear, / With hearts too full for utterance, with but a silent tear."

In the Midwest, a few newspapers were forced to close because so many of their employees signed up. In Connecticut, Elias Howe Jr. — whose income from his family's sewing-machine factories was said to be a quarter of a million dollars a year — attracted wide attention when he publicly proclaimed his dedication to the Union by signing on as a private. Author Nathaniel Hawthorne, traveling in Maine, reported that everywhere he went "the country was astir with volunteers." Each recruit was entitled to a federal bounty of $100 cash. In addition, states, local communities and even businesses commonly offered bounties to volunteers. In the first year of the War, these rewards could amount to $500 — regal sums that drew thousands of men to the colors; later, bounties would mount even higher.

Yet by early August 1862, the enlistment rate had fallen off sharply. Indeed, the initial wave of patriotic fervor lasted only until the wounded began to return in shockingly large numbers from the battlefronts. The staggering casualty lists, a dispiriting string of Union defeats, the newspaper reports of suffering and neglect in Army hospitals — all

Philadelphia's Independence Square serves as a temporary tenting ground for Pennsylvania militia volunteers in 1861. Such improvised bivouacs sprouted up in a number of Northern cities during the War's first year as patriotic fervor prompted more than 620,000 men to enlist in the Union Army. Pennsylvania alone supplied almost 80,000 men.

had a profoundly sobering effect on public opinion. The pine boxes of the dead lay in rail terminals throughout the North — returned "to the village burying ground," as the poet Emily Dickinson wrote, where they "never dreamed of sleeping."

Though the troop calls of May and July 1862 provided more than 400,000 men, the recruits came slowly and Federal officials grew discouraged. When the Administration called for another 300,000 that August, Congress took the unprecedented step of authorizing a draft to fill out the quota of any state that fell short of its requirement. The draft would be managed by the states under their militia powers. All able-bodied men between 18 and 45 would be enrolled by local authorities as militiamen and subject to call.

The real goal of the militia draft was to stimulate volunteer enlistments. Guidelines furnished by the War Department exempted judges, telegraph operators, railroad engineers, skilled munitions workers in public arsenals and certain other government employees. The states could also excuse men with disabilities. Various state rules exempted those afflicted with heart or lung disease, hemorrhoids or chronic diarrhea, hernia, "loss or imperfect vision of the right eye" — presumably the rifle-sighting eye — loss of the front teeth and molars, or "loss of more than one finger of the right or more than two fingers of the left hand." After eliminating the medically unfit and occupationally exempt, the local draft officer was to subtract the number of volunteers from his quota to determine how many men to draft; if the total of volunteers met or exceeded the quota, no draft was held. But if the number was less than the quota, the final step was a lottery — a drawing of names from a wheel or box.

A draftee still had the option of volunteering before he was finally mustered into service as a conscript. By doing so he could avoid the onus of compulsory service, collect a bounty and choose his own regiment. Or a draftee might avoid service entirely by providing a substitute to go in his place. This provision inevitably led to abuses that would get worse as the War progressed.

Within weeks of the announcement of the draft, professional brokers appeared, intent on providing substitutes for a fee. Soon the competition for substitutes became so intense that the brokers took to searching for candidates in slums and waterfront taverns. There they found men who made a profession of first enlisting as a substitute, then deserting and selling their services to another client or broker. Even amateurs could do well in the trade if they were quick-witted. One college student in Connecticut sold himself as a substitute for $300, then contrived to find a $200 replacement for himself even as he was standing in the enlistment line.

Harried draft officials soon found themselves trying to cope with another brand of entrepreneur, "bounty jumpers" — men who enlisted to collect the federal and local bounties for volunteers, and then fled to another town to repeat the process. Equally vexing were the hordes of men who tried to avoid the draft by claiming disabilities. "The prospect of involuntary service," noted the New York *Illustrated News* wryly, "develops an amount of latent diseases and physical disabilities that are perfectly surprising."

Some men maimed themselves by cutting off an index finger or extracting their teeth, while others consulted obliging physicians. A certain Dr. Beckwith of Litchfield, Connecticut, became notorious for the alacrity

The 7th New York Militia boards a train for Washington on April 19, 1861. The 7th had mustered 991 volunteers within a week of the attack on Fort Sumter.

with which he issued certificates of unfitness at $35 apiece. Men who did not happen to know such an accommodating physician could apply to one of the many firms set up to provide fraudulent doctor's certificates.

As a general rule, an exemption was available to anybody who could pay for it. In one recorded case in Fairfield, Connecticut, 62 men were drafted to fill the town's quota. Taken to New Haven for physical examinations, they were all declared fit for service. When they got back to Fairfield, five of them bought substitutes for prices ranging from $300 to $500. The remaining 57 bought medical exemptions for $75 apiece.

So blatant did draft evasion become that the press in many towns took to shaming the draft dodgers by publishing columns of names of exempted men, along with their alleged disabilities. An Iowa newspaper headed one such column the "Coward List." Despite such pressure, the evasions continued, and became even more numerous.

Many who for one reason or another were unable to hire a substitute or get a medical exemption packed up and fled to Canada or Europe. The practice, known as "skedaddling," proved so popular that Secretary Stanton issued orders forbidding potential draftees to leave the country. The New York *Illustrated News* delightedly reported the seizure of a draft evader clad in a dress on a train bound for Niagara Falls. New York police halted men boarding steamers for Europe and turned back those without passports.

Many draft officers began to encounter violent resistance — an ominous sign of greater troubles to come. In Port Washington, Wisconsin, it took eight companies of troops to restore order after a mob carrying a banner reading "No Draft" sacked a recruit-

ing office and threw an enrollment officer down a flight of stairs. Enrollers were spat upon, beaten, scalded with hot water and in some cases shot.

When the final tally was in, the troop calls of the summer of 1862 had yielded 509,000 new recruits, the great majority of them volunteers. The draft's contribution to this harvest was minimal: Wisconsin, for example, inducted 1,739 men, Indiana 742, Connecticut only 44. The majority of the men whose

SCENE, FIFTH AVENUE.

HE. "Ah! Dearest ADDIE! I've succeeded. I've got a Substitute!"
SHE. "Have you? What a curious coincidence! And *I* have found one FOR YOU!"

In an 1862 cartoon, a young woman spurns a suitor who evaded that year's draft by hiring a substitute to serve in his place. Despite such ridicule, the practice was common. In the draft held in the summer of 1863, more than 26,000 of those selected bought substitutes.

names were drawn either volunteered, failed to report, or secured exemptions.

The 1862 draft was viewed as a wasteful and clumsy experiment. Federal officials, unhappy with the frequent postponements and numerous exemptions allowed by the states, concluded that any future draft would have to be run from Washington. It was also generally believed that volunteering was just about played out. Only a well-organized national draft, un-American as it might seem, would provide the necessary manpower. It soon became clear that the Union was going

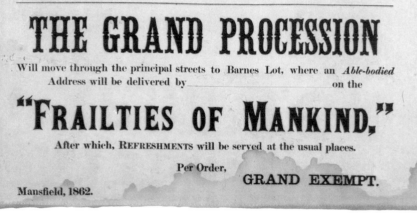

Lampooning the men who evaded military service through dubious medical exemptions, a poster printed in Mansfield, Massachusetts, announces a "Grand Procession" of "Toothless Gummers," "Varicose Cadets" and others claiming absurd disabilities.

to need hundreds of thousands more troops before the War could be won: Losses incurred in September at Antietam and in December at Fredericksburg were devastating to the Army of the Potomac.

In response, a federal conscription law — which took the draft machinery out of the hands of the states — was introduced in Congress early in 1863. It constituted perhaps the strongest assault yet on the steadily eroding tenets of state sovereignty. Democrats, outnumbered in both houses, argued vehe-

mently against the bill, especially because of the provision that set up a network of federal provost marshals in the states to enforce the draft. The law, said a Democratic Congressman from Pennsylvania, was "oppressive, unjust and unconstitutional."

Among other provisions, the bill called for the enrollment of all males between 20 and 45, with bachelors in that age group to be called first, followed by married men between 20 and 25. A house-by-house census of the manpower pool would determine the quotas for each state and district. The call was for 300,000 men. The physically unfit were again exempted, and this time, so were the insane — a provision that one Pennsylvania editor remarked was "unquestionably for the benefit of the abolitionists, who are all crazy as March hares."

Draftees were to serve for three years. But they still had the option of providing a substitute to go in their place. And they were now provided with a new loophole: They could be excused from service if they paid a $300 "commutation fee." The government defended the principle of commutation — and also the provision for substitutes — as necessary concessions to men with jobs or responsibilities too important to abandon.

Republican Senator Henry Wilson, the draft bill's chief sponsor in the Senate, conceded that it was important "for the nation to feel that we throw a dragnet over the country and take up the rich and the poor and put the burden upon all." But when Democratic Senator Milton S. Latham pointed out that this principle was undermined by the existence of loopholes favoring the well-to-do, his argument went unheeded.

For all the controversy, the Senate passed the bill after one long day and night of de-

bate. The House followed suit after four days of debate.

As soon as enrollment began, it was clear that the draft would be both an administrative nightmare and a blow to morale on the home front. The draft machinery was never adequate for the task. California and Oregon, for example, were simply too far away and too sparsely populated for the establishment of efficient draft procedures. In more populous areas, there were not nearly enough enrollment boards or examining physicians to handle the flow of draftees.

From the first, state authorities complained that the quotas imposed on them by Washington were unfair. Governor Joseph A. Gilmore of New Hampshire went so far as to warn the federal government that it "must send a regiment" of infantry if it wished to enforce the quotas assigned his state. Beyond that, both the states and individuals repeatedly questioned whether the federal draft was Constitutional. Some claimed that the conscription act infringed upon powers reserved to the states by making state militiamen eligible for the draft. On this basis, a group of conscripts in Pennsylvania brought suit against a local draft board and won a ruling from the Pennsylvania supreme court that the draft was, in fact, unconstitutional and must be halted at once in the state. The federal government at first ignored the ruling and later contrived to get it reversed.

Many communities were troubled by the inequities of the law and sought to subvert it. Some offered bounties to lure men from outside the district or state who could then enlist and be counted toward the town's quota.

Town agents roamed widely in their efforts to attract volunteers. The residents of Cortland, New York, for example, sent an agent to the occupied South, as the Cortland *Democrat* reported it, "to catch and bring up all the Negroes he can for filling the quota of our town." The agent failed.

Many towns set up funds for men who wished to purchase commutations but were unable to pay the $300 fee. The money for such fees, and for bounties, was generally raised through donations from individuals and businesses or through property taxes.

For some people, the protection thus afforded to local men was a source of civic pride. The Cortland *Democrat* observed in 1864 that the town could pride itself on "having aided in preserving the unity of families intact, snatched unwilling victims from the moloch of war, and added a new link to the chain that binds in one brotherhood all classes in the community." Yet one angry veteran complained to the Hartford *Courant* that the aim of most towns seemed to be "to furnish excuses, not soldiers — to show by some new count of veterans, or some addition of stolen names from another town — or some other iniquitous and shameful means that Hartford, or New Haven, or Barkhamstead, is already far ahead of the quota."

As the War dragged on, the raising of bounty money became an increasingly heavy burden — particularly after the commutation provision was dropped from the draft act in 1864. Neighboring towns and states were forced into financially disastrous competition; in the summer of 1864, the bounties being paid in the area around Cortland soared as high as $900. The inflationary spiral thus touched off could only lead to "enormous debts," warned Ohio Governor John Brough. "There is a payday for it all, either in crushing taxation or dishonor."

Men whose communities could no longer

Coming Home

Cities and towns across the North welcomed home their soldier sons with joyous, flag-waving celebrations. During the first two years of the conflict, when short-term enlistments were common, a near-constant parade of regiments tromped through the rail stations of the home front.

In New York City, for example, the 69th New York returned in July 1861 from the Battle of Bull Run in a burst of patriotic glory. "The windows and roofs were thronged," *Leslie's Illustrated Weekly* reported, "and from every available spot, flags and tokens were displayed."

As the War dragged on and tours of du[ty] lengthened, however, the troop trains a[r]rived less frequently — and with regimen[ts] on board whose ranks had been thinned [by] battle casualties and disease. Increasin[g]ly, the outbursts of joy were underscor[ed] with notes of sadness.

Friends and relatives of the 1st Michigan clamber atop boxcars to glimpse the regiment as it returns home to Detroit on August 2, 1861.

A milling throng in Troy, New York, awaits the arrival of a hometown regiment, the 2nd New York, in May 1863; the regiment's ranks had been reduced recently at the Battle of Chancellorsville.

Broadway unfurls its flags for the returning 69th New York on July 27, 1861. The 90-day unit quickly reformed and reenlisted en masse.

THE DRAFT.

The draft will commence in the 14th Congressional District, on

Thursday, Sept. 17th, 1863,

At 10 o'clock A M., at the Court House in Wooster, Ohio.

The whole number required from this district is SIX HUNDRED AND NINETEEN, to which fifty per cent. will be added to cover exemptions. The following table exhibits the number to be drafted from each sub-district:

HOLMES COUNTY—To the first sub-district, 21; Second, 21; Third, 18; Fourth, 27; Fifth, 12; Sixth, 18; Seventh, 19.

ASHLAND COUNTY—Eighth sub-dist., 24; Ninth, 20; Tenth, 24; Eleventh, 27; Twelfth, 21; Thirteenth, 18; Fourteenth, 24.

WAYNE COUNTY—Fifteenth sub-district, 30; Sixteenth, 25; Seventeenth, 24; Eighteenth, 29; Nineteenth, 30; Twentieth, 23; Twenty-first, 41; Twenty-second, 24.

MEDINA COUNTY—Twenty-third sub-district, 39; twenty-fourth, 19; twenty-fifth, 27; twenty-sixth, 17; twenty-seventh, 19; twenty-eighth, 14; twenty-ninth, 12; thirtieth, 15; thirty-first, 15.

LORAIN COUNTY—32d sub-district, 16; 33d, 26; 34th, 13; 35th, 15; 36th, 29; 37th, 24; 38th, 36; 39th, 15; 40th, 22; 41st, 20; 42d, 16.

The draft will commence with the forty-second sub-district in Lorain county, and end with the first sub-district in Holmes county.

JAMES L. DRAKE,
Wooster, Sept. 11, 1863.   Capt. & Provost Marshal.

An announcement of the draft in an Ohio Congressional district in 1863 lists the number of men to be conscripted from each county and sub-district. The quotas were based on the number of eligible males identified in the areas by a survey.

afford the bounties — and who were too poor themselves to pay for substitutes — were left with little choice. A satirist in New York summarized their plight in a bitter parody of John Gibbons' "Father Abraham" poem: "We're coming, Father Abraham, three hundred thousand more, / We leave our homes and firesides with bleeding hearts and sore, / Since poverty has been our crime, we bow to the decree, / We are the poor who have no wealth to purchase liberty."

Just as disturbing as the inequity of the draft law was the continuing climate of lawlessness it fostered. The powerful New York politician Roscoe Conkling spoke for many concerned citizens when he observed angrily that the draft had degenerated into a "carnival of corrupt disorder and the paradise of coxcombs and thieves."

By 1863, skedaddling had become so commonplace that Connecticut railroads put on extra cars for the droves of men expected to flee the state. It was estimated that 20,000 men skedaddled from Ohio that year alone. They left behind them a choice collection of bounty jumpers — drifters and riffraff from New York, Canada and even Europe.

Some bounty jumpers profited so handsomely that they were able to return home and open their own businesses. Although the penalties for bounty jumping became steadily more severe — until capture could mean execution — there was never a lack of men willing to attempt it. Sometimes they did so en masse: In late 1864, for example, 97 out of 300 recruits fled from a train as it rattled through Ohio. The individual record holder was one John O'Connor, who enlisted and jumped 32 times before he was court-martialed in Albany, New York, and sentenced to four years in prison.

Substitute brokers were so prevalent that some communities sought ways to banish them. These "cormorants," as the New York *Tribune* called them, were on the prowl in all the large cities for men free to take somebody else's place. The brokers necessarily concentrated much of their attention on men who were over the age limit, boys who were under it and unsuspecting aliens of any age. European immigrants were sometimes shanghaied as soon as they stepped ashore, while brokers operating out of Detroit specialized in kidnapping Canadians with the aid of drugs and liquor. Overage derelicts were cleaned up, rested and treated with hair dye so they would look young enough to pass muster. A retarded youth from Troy, New York, was kidnapped, accepted as a substitute and sent to the front, where he was never heard from again — even though his anguished mother met with the President in an effort to find him.

To fight the draft, potential inductees rubbed sand into their eyes to feign conjunctivitis, or smoked and drank heavily before the examination in an effort to produce symptoms of heart disease. Others hired women to pose as their mothers and testify that their "sons" were needed at home. As a last resort, some men tried to bribe draft officials. A provost marshal in Philadelphia was court-martialed for accepting a fee to scratch names off the enrollment list.

Bounty jumpers, reluctant draftees and substitutes bent on desertion were so prevalent by late 1863 that new soldiers were often treated like prisoners of war. When Frank Wilkeson, an eager 16-year-old farm boy from upstate New York, enlisted late that year, he was astonished to find himself confined in a penitentiary with what he described as "eight hundred or one thousand ruffians, closely guarded by heavy lines of sentinels." Some of his fellow recruits and inductees tried to escape by hiding inside mattresses and even garbage bins. When the men marched through Albany, Wilkeson heard no cheers from the watching throng; instead small boys lobbed mud balls at them and cried, "Come see the bounty jumpers." As they prepared to board a steamer in Manhattan, four men broke and ran. Three were immediately shot and killed. The fourth nearly got away, but a tall officer carrying a pistol overtook him. "He made no attempt to arrest the deserter," Wilkeson wrote, "but placed his pistol to the back of the runaway's head and blew his brains out as he ran. That ended all attempts to escape."

Much of the corruption and venality of the draft system was blamed unfairly on the officers who enrolled potential draftees and policed the induction procedure. To take such a job, declared an assembly of Pennsylvania Democrats in 1863, was an act unworthy of any American. The provost marshals were likened to pimps, spies and mad dogs. It was said that they secretly eliminated the names of Administration supporters from the draft wheels so that "the lottery of death" was sure to pick those who opposed the War.

The anger that enrollment officers stirred was expressed in more than words. Two officers were ambushed and murdered as they made their rounds in Rush County, Indiana. Elsewhere in the state, bands of armed men roamed from town to town seizing the enrollment books and threatening the lives of the officers. "We the undersigned will give you our advice for your own good," read a note sent to one enroller. "If you don't lay aside the enrolling, your life will be taken tomorrow night." It was signed "Your Friend." In a tough Chicago district called "the Patch," two enrollment officers were assaulted and seriously injured by a brick-hurling mob. A mining-company official in Pennsylvania was shot to death in his home by assailants who suspected him of giving enrollment officers information about his employees.

The experience of enroller Peter W. Kutz, who covered Pennsylvania's Schuykill County, was not unusual. According to a report by his superior, Kutz testified that he was threatened by a defiant citizen who "would have killed him or broken his bones for him"; Kutz retreated and several men trailed him, menacing him with stones. Kutz, like more than half the state's enrollment officers, resigned to seek safer work.

An even uglier sign of popular anger at conscription was the increasingly open hostility expressed against blacks. The Democratic press skillfully played on the theme that the Northern workingman was betraying his own best interests by fighting to free slaves

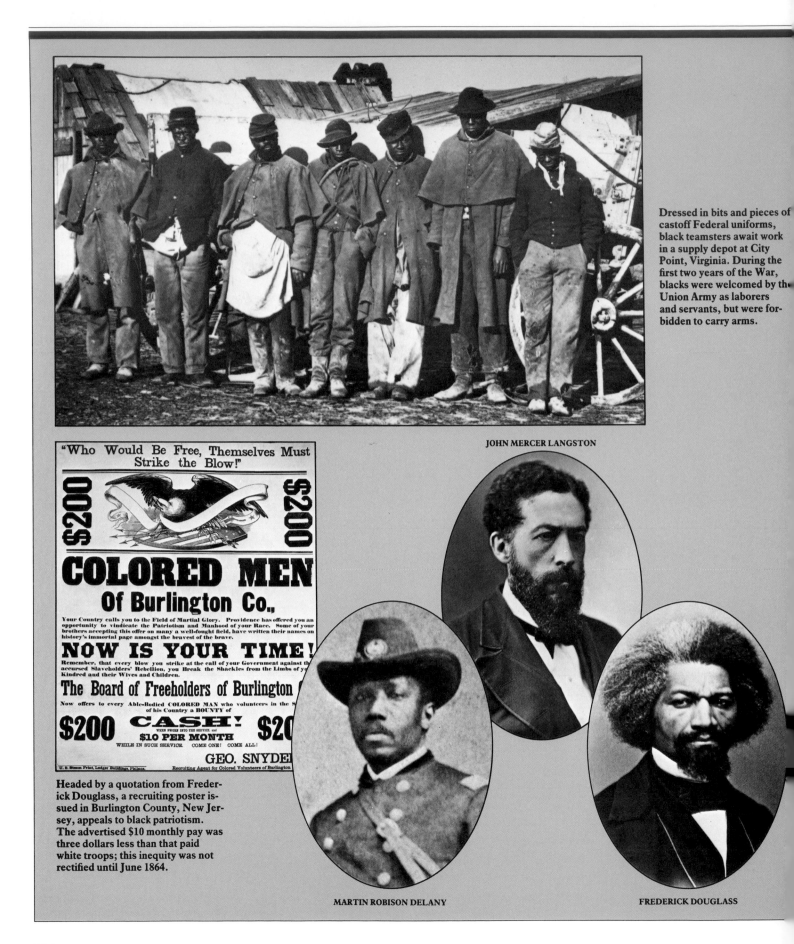

Dressed in bits and pieces of castoff Federal uniforms, black teamsters await work in a supply depot at City Point, Virginia. During the first two years of the War, blacks were welcomed by the Union Army as laborers and servants, but were forbidden to carry arms.

JOHN MERCER LANGSTON

Headed by a quotation from Frederick Douglass, a recruiting poster issued in Burlington County, New Jersey, appeals to black patriotism. The advertised $10 monthly pay was three dollars less than that paid white troops; this inequity was not rectified until June 1864.

"Who Would Be Free, Themselves Must Strike the Blow!"

$200 $200

COLORED MEN
Of Burlington Co.,

Your Country calls you to the Field of Martial Glory. Providence has offered you an opportunity to vindicate the Patriotism and Manhood of your Race. Some of your brothers accepting this offer on many a well-fought field, have written their names on history's immortal page amongst the bravest of the brave.

NOW IS YOUR TIME!

Remember, that every blow you strike at the call of your Government against the accursed Slaveholders' Rebellion, you Break the Shackles from the Limbs of your Kindred and their Wives and Children.

The Board of Freeholders of Burlington

Now offers to every Able-Bodied COLORED MAN who volunteers in the Service of his Country a BOUNTY of

$200 CASH! $200
WHEN SWORN INTO THE SERVICE, and
$10 PER MONTH
WHILE IN SUCH SERVICE.   COME ONE!   COME ALL!

GEO. SNYDER,
U. S. Steam Print, Ledger Buildings, Philada.   Recruiting Agent for Colored Volunteers of Burlington

MARTIN ROBISON DELANY

FREDERICK DOUGLASS

Black Troops to Defend the Union

When President Lincoln authorized the full-scale recruitment of black soldiers late in 1862, the three great black leaders whose portraits appear opposite embarked on a mission to sign up entire black regiments for the Federal armies. The presence of blacks in the ranks would surely elevate the race, they reasoned. Nobody could ever deny full citizenship, Frederick Douglass declared, to a man who had had "an eagle on his button, a musket on his shoulder."

John Langston, a self-educated Virginia attorney who later became a law school dean and college president, traveled through the Midwest, signing up recruits and sending them to Massachusetts, where the first two officially authorized black regiments were organized and trained. The equally remarkable Martin Delany, a largely self-taught physician who was later commissioned an infantry major, covered much of the same territory, recruiting and also checking the enlistees' health. Douglass, the most eloquent 19th Century spokesman for blacks, sought out candidates in New York and other localities.

Once the rolls of the 54th and 55th Massachusetts had been filled, the three men continued raising recruits for regiments organized in Ohio, Pennsylvania, Connecticut and other states. In part because of their efforts, black men made up almost 10 per cent of all those to wear the Union blue during the War.

The men of the 26th U.S. Colored Infantry form for review in sharply ordered ranks at Pennsylvania's Camp William Penn in 1865.

who would inevitably "fill the shops, yards and other places of labor" and "compel us to compete with them for the support of our families." It followed, said the Meadville, Pennsylvania, *Crawford Democrat,* that the workers of the North were "willing to fight for Uncle Sam," but not "for Uncle Sambo."

In fact, few Northern laboring men had any personal experience of blacks or any knowledge of how they lived or thought, but like most whites they expressed an ingrained dislike of them. Despite the emotional impact of the Emancipation Proclamation, blacks were as rigorously excluded from white life in 1863 as they had been before the War. When the black abolitionist leader Frederick Douglass visited wartime Philadelphia, he observed that the city had "its white schools and colored schools, its white churches and its colored churches, its white Christianity and its colored Christianity."

Another witness who saw the situation keenly from the inside was John Rock, a black justice of the peace in Massachusetts. "Few seem to comprehend our position in the free states," he observed. "The masses seem to think that we are oppressed only in the South. This is a mistake; we are oppressed everywhere in this slavery-cursed land." Even in the abolitionist stronghold of Massachusetts, he noted, "while colored men have many rights, they have few privileges." Among the privileges they were denied, he added wryly, was the right to lie in white graveyards.

The racial chasm in Northern life that Douglass and Rock knew so well also impressed the English journalist Edward Dicey. "I have often wondered," he wrote, "at how very little the Americans I met with seemed to know about the negroes who lived amongst them." Blacks were not only physically segregated in urban ghettos but sealed off by walls of myth and misunderstanding. In the ghettos blacks developed their own churches, schools, and societies for the aid of the penniless and sick. Often, they conversed, sang and told stories in a dialect that whites found hard to fathom.

Whites rarely ventured into the older black ghettos and almost never set foot in the newer shantytowns crowded with blacks who had fled north in the wake of the Union armies. One exception, a white who in 1864 visited the tar-paper huts and rat-infested alleys of a swampy black slum in Washington known as Murder Bay, described the plight of its inhabitants: "The weather is cold; they have little or no wood. Snow covers the ground, and they have a scanty supply of rags called clothes. The hospital is crowded with the sick. Government gives them a very, *very* small allowance of soup. Ninety gallons was given yesterday; but what is that to feed thousands of families." Many, he feared, would die. And he added: "The feeling against them, among many in this place, is bitter, malignant, devilish."

The presence of such shantytowns intensified the worst fears of Northern white workers that their jobs would soon be in jeopardy. And the workers had a further grudge: When they went out on strike to protest low wages, employers often broke the strike by replacing them with blacks. Inevitably, the fears and frustrations of the workers led to hard feelings and ultimately to violence.

In the summer of 1862, a mob assaulted a Brooklyn tobacco factory where 25 black men, women and children worked. After the blacks barricaded themselves inside, the mob tried unsuccessfully to burn the building down. There was similar mob violence in half a dozen Northern cities — including Detroit, where several blacks were killed and 200 left homeless.

Longshoremen, whose employment was sporadic in the best of times, were particularly sensitive to black competition. When blacks in Cincinnati were hired as stevedores on Ohio River boats in July 1862, the homes of blacks were set afire and a special posse of 100 men had to be raised to keep the peace. When shippers in Buffalo hired blacks to handle cargoes, three blacks were killed and 12 brutally beaten. White longshoremen in New York blamed the failure of a strike in the early spring of 1863 on the black workers who replaced them. Black longshoremen were similarly blamed for breaking strikes on the waterfronts of Brooklyn, Boston, Cleveland, Detroit and Chicago.

When the federal draft commenced in the summer of 1863, resentment at draft inequities combined with hostility toward blacks to create enormous urban tensions. White workingmen listened to firebrands like Democratic Congressman Samuel S. Cox of Ohio, who warned that the result of their serving in the Army would be to find "Negroes filling their places" on the job.

The tension reached a breaking point in the city of New York. With its struggling immigrant groups massed in rundown tenements, New York was a tinderbox awaiting a spark. New York's working-class Irish, in particular, were seething at the erosion of their buying power brought on by wartime inflation, and outraged at the use of blacks to replace striking Irish longshoremen. To make matters worse, the antiwar movement had in New York some of its most impassioned spokesmen, including former mayor

Fernando Wood, who had once proposed that the city leave the Union rather than lose Southern trade. New York's Democratic Governor, Horatio Seymour, had inveighed in a recent message to the legislature against the "inequality and injustice" of a law compelling reluctant draftees to serve.

As the federal draft began, most of the New York City militia units that could have been called on to keep the peace at home were at the front in Pennsylvania. The protective force available in the city consisted of the regular police, a small number of soldiers on duty in the harbor garrisons, and a few soldiers of the Invalid Corps — disabled veterans fit only for guard duty.

The first 1,236 names were drawn from a wheel on Saturday, July 11, after which the drawing was suspended until Monday the 13th. On Sunday, the names of the drafted men appeared in the morning papers at the same time that casualty lists from Gettysburg were being posted around town.

The police got word shortly after 9 a.m. on Monday that gangs of men and boys, many armed with crowbars and clubs, were roaming the streets. The mobs converged on the 9th District draft office at Third Avenue and 46th Street, where the drawing was proceeding under the guard of an uneasy force of 60 policemen led by 19th Precinct Captain G. T. Porter. Suddenly there was a pistol shot, and the crowd unleashed a volley of stones. Porter's men held off the mob long enough for the draft officials to escape, and then retreated. The crowd stormed inside, and within minutes the office and the adjoining buildings were in flames. The rioters then broke into nearby houses and shops, launching an orgy of looting and destruction.

Police Superintendent John Kennedy,

hurrying to the scene from headquarters on Mulberry Street, was spotted by a group of rioters and was clubbed to the sidewalk. When he came to and tried to run, he was caught and beaten again.

The rioters continued to surge through the streets. A 32-man detachment of the Invalid Corps tried to halt them by firing a ragged volley, but the mob attacked with clubs and paving stones and routed the disabled men, killing two of them and wounding 15.

To a New York *Times* reporter, the rioters resembled "demons, the men being more or less intoxicated, dirty and half-clothed." Women and children trailed behind them.

On Lexington Avenue, Wall Street lawyer George Templeton Strong watched as a horde pillaged two three-story houses. Strong — who in August 1864 would pay a young Dutchman $1,100 to serve as his substitute — reacted to this ragged band of draft rioters with patrician disdain. "Every brute in the drove was pure Celtic — hod carrier or loafer," he wrote. "Paving-stones began to fly at the windows, ladies and children emerged from the rear and had a rather hard scramble over a high board fence, and then scudded off across the open, Heaven knows whither. Then men and small boys appeared at rear windows and began smashing the sashes and the blinds and shied out light articles, such as books and crockery. At last a light smoke began to float out of the windows and I came away."

The outnumbered police could only manage piecemeal shows of force. A wedge of 44 officers charged the mob moving southward on Third Avenue and drove them back temporarily. But the mob came surging on, augmented by laborers pouring out of shops and factories into the sweltering July heat. It was the kind of day, one observer said, that "makes you feel as if you had washed yourself in molasses and water."

The city's board of aldermen held an emergency meeting and discussed raising $3.7 million to pay the commutation fees for New York draftees. But the rioters knew nothing of this, and the Third Avenue mob, now three to five thousand strong, moved on to an armory at 21st Street and Second Avenue, where about 1,000 rifles were stored. Only a block away, 3,000 additional carbines and muskets were to be found at the Union Steam Works, a factory that would survive several abortive attacks.

Thirty-four policemen, members of the elite Broadway Squad, had been sent to protect the armory, and they held the rock-throwing crowd at bay for an hour and a half. But when no reinforcements arrived, the officers were finally ordered to evacuate through a rear window. The rioters swarmed inside, began seizing weapons, and set the building afire. More police finally reached the scene and scattered the mob, but only temporarily. The death toll for the battle at the armory came to 13, some of whom perished in the burning building.

It soon became clear that blacks were particular targets of the mob's wrath. While the crowd on Second Avenue was setting the armory ablaze, another crowd at Fifth Avenue and 43rd Street was attacking an orphanage for black children. The 237 youngsters who lived there, all under the age of 12, were led out a back door to safety as the mob outside screamed, "Burn the niggers' nest." A few minutes later the rioters broke in and began ransacking the building, then set it on fire. The frenzied crowd blocked firemen trying to douse the flames, and cut their hoses.

Rioters pursue a black famil[y]
through vacant lots off Lexington Avenue, on Manha[t]-
tan's East Side, scene [of]
much of the worst violenc[e.]

On July 14, 1863, a frenzied
mob of draft rioters in
New York stones to death
Colonel Henry O'Brien,
leader of a detachment of
volunteers that tried to
quell the violence.

The Orphan Asylum for Colored Children goes up in
flames as rioters carry off
furniture plundered from
the buildings. The procession of vandals lugging away
such stolen goods was
said to have stretched 10
blocks down Fifth Avenue.

A Negro cart driver is hanged from a tree and his body burned on Clarkson Street in Greenwich Village, home to a number of blacks.

A portion of the roving mob sacks Brooks Brothers, a well-known clothing store then on Catherine Street.

A hero of the Draft Riots, Colonel Cleveland Winslow was in New York when the violence began. He swiftly rounded up a force of volunteers, mostly discharged veterans, armed them with weapons found in a city arsenal, and led them against the mobs until regular troops arrived.

Elsewhere in the city, gangs of men began to assault blacks wherever they encountered them. One William Jones was walking home in Greenwich Village when he was spotted by a band of rioters. They grabbed the hapless man and hanged him from a tree, then lit a bonfire under his corpse. Peter Heuston, a Mohawk Indian who had served in the Mexican War, was taken for a black and beaten so badly that he later died in Bellevue Hospital. More than 700 blacks eventually took refuge at police headquarters, while others fled to Long Island, New Jersey and upper Manhattan. Many stores that employed blacks were forced to close. One store that remained open hung out a sign to appease the crowd: "No Niggers in the Rear."

The beleaguered police finally got some help when several militia units, along with a number of veterans and soldiers home on leave, reported for duty Monday night. That evening, rioters attacked Horace Greeley's prodraft *Tribune* and tore up the ground floor before being driven off by a massive police assault. George Templeton Strong wired President Lincoln asking for troops and a declaration of martial law. And Edward Sanford of the U.S. Military Telegraph Service reported to Secretary of War Stanton that "New York is tonight at the mercy of a mob."

The battle between the mob and the lawmen for control of the city teetered back and forth throughout the day on Tuesday. Three hundred policemen were ambushed at Second Avenue and 34th Street by people hurling bricks from windows and rooftops, but the officers rallied and entered the buildings in pursuit of the rioters. A 150-man detachment of the 11th New York Volunteers, led by Colonel Henry O'Brien, held an unruly crowd at bay by firing over their heads, but the volley accidentally killed a two-year-old girl watching from an upper-story window. Later, recognizing O'Brien as the officer whose men had killed the little girl, a furious crowd beat him and tortured him with fire until he was dead. Elsewhere a white woman named Ann Derrickson, the wife of a black man, was beaten to death by a mob while trying to save her son Alfred, whose clothes had been doused with kerosene. Earlier that day, Governor Seymour had arrived in the city and made a much-criticized speech in which he referred to the rioters as "my friends" and promised to use

Company G of the 7th New York Militia pauses near a Manhattan intersection while patrolling the city in the aftermath of the Draft Riots. The regiment, which had been on garrison duty in Maryland, was recalled to help stem the violence.

his influence to have the draft suspended.

Savage fighting raged during the day at the Union Steam Works on Second Avenue, where several hundred police and infantrymen were repeatedly attacked by rioters bent on seizing the carbines stored inside. Flailing their clubs, the police finally drove the mob back and spirited the weapons away in a wagon. On Pitt Street, troops encountered a crowd carrying signs reading "No Draft." When the protesters charged, the soldiers fired, killing eight and wounding four.

The riot has begun to take on the character of a class war, as toughs set upon well-dressed men with the cry, "There goes a $300 man." In Washington, meanwhile, five regiments, including New York's famous 7th, were ordered to the embattled city.

The mob continued to control scattered sections of Manhattan through Wednesday despite the gradual arrival of more troops and a premature proclamation by Mayor George Opdyke that the riot was over (troops were exchanging fire with musket-wielding rioters on Third Avenue at about the time that Opdyke was proclaiming peace in the streets). Novelist Herman Melville, watching the action from a rooftop that day, could still plainly hear "the Atheist roar of riot."

At 6 p.m., Colonel Cleveland Winslow

and a 150-man force of ex-soldiers blasted 10 rounds of canister from two howitzers down First Avenue at a threatening mob. Winslow's men cleared the street, but were forced to retreat when fired upon from the rooftops. The city remained a place of terror for blacks: Abraham Franklin, a crippled coachman, was dragged from his home on Seventh Avenue and hanged from a lamppost by a mob cheering "Jefferson Davis."

By Thursday morning, the riot was at last sputtering out. Word spread that the Army's provost marshal, General James B. Fry, had sent a message from Washington temporarily suspending the draft in the city. The veterans of the New York 7th had arrived in town shortly before dawn; by the end of the day, more than 4,000 soldiers were in the city.

The hard-core rioters made a final stand on Thursday afternoon near Gramercy Park. After an 80-man troop of dismounted cavalrymen was routed by a barrage of gunfire, reinforcements arrived and cleared the buildings of snipers, pursuing them through hallways and over rooftops. The mob in the street fell back as the troops charged in and took prisoners. The riot was over.

The four days of violence left 119 people dead and 306 injured; property damage ran to $1.5 million. As calm was restored, New York resembled an occupied city. When the draft was resumed a month later, 43 regiments were stationed in the vicinity. The drawing was completed without further disturbance.

Antidraft uprisings on a much smaller scale flared up in several other Northeastern cities and towns. The most serious was in Boston, where a mob of about 5,000 attacked the Cooper Street armory on the evening of July 14. Troops fired into the crowd with rifles and cannon, killing a number of people. In Troy, New York, more than 300 protesters destroyed the offices of the Troy *Daily Times* and then marched on a black church. Before they reached their target, however, they were halted by a courageous priest and persuaded to disperse.

Long after the tumult in the streets and the angry debates came the final test of the 1863 draft — the number of men it yielded. By that measure, the draft was more than disappointing: It was disastrous. To begin with, about 13 per cent of the 292,441 men called failed to report. Of those who showed up to be examined, a staggering 65 per cent received exemptions, nearly half of them on physical grounds — a pattern that would be repeated in later calls. The number "held in service" was 88,171. Of these, just under 60 per cent paid the $300 commutation fee. The 1863 draft call thus netted a total of 35,883 men. All but 9,881 of them were substitutes.

General George G. Meade, Commander of the Army of the Potomac, had held that "the crisis of this revolution" would turn on the success or failure of the draft. Now he pronounced it "a failure." Not only were the numbers far below expectations, but the men themselves, Meade said, were "mostly worthless."

Three subsequent draft calls — those in the spring and fall of 1864 and the spring of 1865 — were no more successful. Of all the soldiers credited to the Union armies during the War, less than 2.5 per cent were men called in the draft. Another 5 per cent or so were hired substitutes. The rest were volunteers of one kind or another; the records do not show how many of these were bounty

An 1862 Christmas painting evokes the loneliness and heartaches brought by the War. As her children dream of Santa Claus *(top left)*, a soldier's wife prays for her husband, who is seen at right in a bleak winter encampment gazing on pictures of his loved ones. The painting's bottom border shows troops slogging through snow, soldiers' graves and a ship tossing in a wintry sea.

jumpers. General James Fry was on the mark when he said that the conscription act was "essentially a law not to secure military service but to exempt men from it."

Was the price too high? Certainly, no single aspect of the War so bitterly divided the Northern home front, or released such murderous hatreds. The editor of the Washington *Sunday Times* was not far wrong when he wrote in the riot-plagued summer of 1863 that the "nation is at this time in a state of revolution, North, South, East and West."

Yet for all its imperfections, the draft nevertheless provided the necessary spur to volunteering when volunteering had all but ceased. Without conscription, said General William T. Sherman, there would have been no way to "separate the sheep from the goats and demonstrate what citizens will fight and what will only talk." As it happened, great

numbers of Northern men were willing to fight. In 1863 several states, among them Ohio, Illinois, Indiana and New Jersey, provided so many volunteers that they did not have to draft. A total of 83,242 recruits enlisted during the first nine months of the year. And the pace picked up: In the final two years of the War, more than a million men volunteered. From Fort Sumter to Appomattox, more than two million men enlisted voluntarily to fight for the Union.

It was the spirit of the volunteer that contributed to an emerging American nationalism. There may have been dissenters, and violent ones, but there was also a growing sense of national honor and duty. At its best, this patriotic energy was expressed not only in preparations for war but in the growth of charitable and relief activities whose scope was as wide as the country itself.

BOY IN FANCY FORAGE CAP

OFFICER AND SON IN MILITARY GARB

YOUNG GIRL CARRYING FLAG

CHILD IN MILITARY-STYLE SUIT

112

The Children's War

From the start, the War inflamed the fertile imaginations of children across the land. Sustained by patriotic feeling and romantic notions, child warriors were everywhere: The most spirited of the Lincoln children, Tad, eight years old when the War began, swaggered about the White House in a scaled-down officer's uniform, brandishing a sword. The lad signed his name "Col. Tad L."

The youthful fixation on war created a vast industry in children's uniforms, toy firearms, drums and other accouter-ments for play-acting. When enthusiasm for the colorful Zouave regiments ran high in the early months of the War, there was a huge demand for children's Zouave jackets and dolls. The steady sale of toy drums (there were five drum manufacturers in Massachusetts alone) was fueled by tales of heroic drummer boys who served with the Union armies. Even educational publishers profited — by bringing out jingoistic spelling books printed on cloth so durable as to make patriotism virtually indestructible.

TAD LINCOLN IN OFFICER'S UNIFORM

CHILD IN ZOUAVE OUTFIT

BOY IN MILITARY CAP

GIRL IN MILITARY CAP WITH DRUM

TOY CAVALRY SABER

PAPIER-MÂCHÉ ZOUAVE SOLDIERS

CHILD'S CAVALRY KEPI

CHINA DOLL IN PATRIOTIC GOWN

SCALED-DOWN REGULATION DRUM

CHILD'S ZOUAVE UNIFORM AND FEZ

PATRIOTIC PRIMER ON CLOTH

THE UNION

A is America,
...nd of the free.

C is a Captain,
who led on his men.

...a Battle,
our soldiers did see.

D is a Drummer
Boy, called little Bon...

"An Artery of Love"

"If this war has developed some of the most brutal, bestial and devilish qualities lurking in the human race, it has also shown us how much of the angel there is in the best men and women."

MARY LIVERMORE, U.S. SANITARY COMMISSION ORGANIZER

4

R. C. Gridley, a merchant in the rich and boisterous mining town of Austin in the Nevada Territory, was a man who honored his word. Having sworn that he would carry a 20-pound sack of flour a mile through town if he lost a bet on a local election, he emerged from his store on April 20, 1864, bearing the sack on his shoulder. He found that a crowd had gathered there to accompany him, and a band as well.

The procession grew noisier and more festive as Gridley progressed. By the time he reached the far side of town, one mile from where he had started, his followers were eager to toast his success. They crowded into a local tavern — where Gridley had an inspiration.

He proposed that they auction off the sack of flour and turn the proceeds over to the United States Sanitary Commission — the enormous private relief agency that funneled medical and other supplies and services to the Union's soldiers. This would be a different kind of auction, however: Each successive bidder would buy the sack only to return it to the auctioneer. That way, it could be sold over and over again, as long as the bids kept coming.

Gridley immediately pledged $200. Somebody else shouted that he was in for $350. In the next hour, a score of men bought and returned the sack. By the time the tavern closed that day, the total take stood at better than $4,000.

Buoyed by that success, Gridley and his friends decided to take the sack on the road. They quickly sold and resold it for $6,000 at a mining camp near the rich Comstock Lode. In Virginia City, it brought $13,000. Across the Sierras in Sacramento and San Francisco, it picked up another $5,000. Eventually, Gridley and his friends took it as far east as St. Louis. When its much-publicized travels were over, it had earned more than $70,000 for the Sanitary Commission.

The Austin sack of flour represented a phenomenon occurring across the Union — the energetic efforts of civilians to organize in support of the fighting men. In ambition and scale, this campaign exceeded anything ever attempted by a people at war. The vast sums raised by the Sanitary Commission and other voluntary agencies supported dozens of programs that provided for the soldiers' comfort and sometimes for their safety. The people at home gave not only money but food and clothing in staggering quantities. Women went into the hospitals and even onto the battlefields to care for the wounded. Small wonder that a Sanitary Commission official was moved to call the relief effort "an artery of the people's love to the people's army."

The civilian effort was crucial, and it was prompted largely by the inadequacies of the federal government in providing for the troops. Nothing in the experience of the bureaucracy in Washington had prepared it for total war or the needs of a large army. As civilians moved to supply those needs, they

116

were gradually compelled to enlarge their views and look beyond community and state. Soldiers' aid became a prime force for unifying the nation.

In the first months of the War, however, both individual and community efforts focused on support of local military units. Indeed, many communities set up aid societies to care for local regiments as soon as they were mustered into service.

The aid was often essential. During the spring of 1861, when the Army's makeshift commissary service was overwhelmed by the flood of new recruits, many regiments would have been on starvation rations had it not been for food from home. Prominent local citizens not only gathered the donations but arranged for their transport and accompanied the supplies to the camps.

A good Samaritan from Hartford named Virgil Cornish traveled to military hospitals with diverse items, including stationery, stamps, bitters, smelling salts, liquid rennet, cologne, oranges and pickles. Although he intended these articles as gifts for Connecticut soldiers only, he found that he could not ignore needy soldiers from other states. His reward, he recalled, was that many of the sick and wounded greeted him with a cry of "Good for Connecticut!" when he made his rounds.

In homes, in churches and in schools, volunteers knitted socks and sewed shirts (one group in Boston produced a thousand shirts in a day) and packed books and provisions to send to the troops. Most women, recalled the Chicago volunteer Mary Livermore, worked independently — unaware of what others were doing but fired with a determination to have "a hand or a foot or an eye or a voice on the side of freedom." Heed-

ing a plea for bandage materials, volunteers scraped tons of lint from cloth. Soon it was piled high in lint depots across the North; there was not enough transport and labor to convert it all into bandages.

Somehow the idea spread that soldiers bound for the Southern states needed to wear havelocks — cloth head-and-neck coverings named after the British general who invented them for use in the tropics as protection against the sun. Sewing circles produced havelocks by the thousands, until word got back that the bewildered troops were wearing them as nightcaps.

Other groups concentrated on less exotic articles of dress: Boston had its Slipper Circle and its Handkerchief Circle, while New York had its Ladies' Military Blue Stocking Association, which reported that it had knit 1,292 pairs of regulation blue stockings in its first three months. Much was made of the fact that a 10-year-old girl in Cleveland had made 229 towels, and that a 93-year-old woman in Duxbury, Massachusetts, was knitting worsted stockings just as she had as a child for Washington's suffering troops at Valley Forge.

Groups of young women formed themselves into Alert Clubs to solicit donations of clothing, which groups of boys calling themselves Minute Men then collected in wheelbarrows and wagons. The children of New Haven were reported to have raised $730 through a "Boys' and Girls' Fourth of July Fruit Fund," which solicited money for fresh fruit for the troops in place of the traditional fireworks. In Bavaria, Ohio, a group of boys called the Sawbuck Rangers began sawing firewood for the wives of men who had enlisted, and the farmers of Windham County, Connecticut, banded together to get

in the harvest for a soldier's wife. Compassionate physicians refused to send bills to the widows of those killed in action. Every Thanksgiving and Christmas, citizens' committees in many Northern towns dispatched tons of turkey and dressing to the soldiers of their local regiments.

In this fever of activity, the women of the North displayed a gritty determination that was often expressed in fiercely anti-Confederate terms. The British journalist George Augustus Sala reported that women had become "the bitterest, most vengeful of politicians," and that there was an "implacability" in their attitudes toward the enemy. To Jane Stuart Woolsey of New York, the War was dreadful, but it was better than a "hollow and hateful peace" with the Confederate "mutineers." In a letter to a Parisian friend, she struck a patriotic note: "Inside the parlor windows the atmosphere has been very fluffy since Sumter, with lint-making and the tearing of endless lengths of flannel and cotton bandages and cutting out of innumerable garments. It seems as if we never were alive till now; never had a country till now. How could we ever have laughed at Fourth-of-Julys?"

The press spurred Northern women on to further effort by talking of the supposedly greater devotion and sacrifice of Southern wives and mothers. One volunteer indignantly denied that assertion in a tract entitled "A Few Words in Behalf of the Loyal Women in the United States." Southern women, the author insisted, were "bright and fierce" but notoriously "fickle," whereas Northern women were unfailingly "tender and true."

Indeed, the women of the North could be true to a fault. In the first frenzied weeks of

TO THE

Patriotic Women of Philadelphia.

A meeting of the Ladies of the City of Philadelphia will be held this day, at 4 o'clock, P. M., at the School Room, in Tenth Street, one door above Spring Garden St., west side, to devise means to give aid and comfort to our noble Soldiers, who have volunteered for the defence of our outraged Flag.

Contributions will be thankfully accepted of such materials as may be found useful to the Volunteers.

In times like these, when our Husbands, Fathers, Sons and Brothers are doing battle for the honor of our common country, let the women be not behind-hand in bestowing their aid and sympathy.

MANY LADIES.

KING & BAIRD, Printers, 607 Sansom Street, Philada.

the War, there were not nearly enough trains to carry the perishable contributions that came pouring into depots. Chicago's Mary Livermore recalled that housewives "rifled their store-rooms and preserve-closets of canned fruits and pots of jam and marmalade, which they packed with clothing and blankets, books and stationery, photographs and 'comfort bags.' Baggage cars were soon flooded with fermenting sweetmeats, and broken pots of jelly, that ought never to have been sent." Too often, the decaying food had to be thrown out, along with the clothing it was wrapped in.

So uncoordinated were early relief activities that some essential items were in surplus and others almost impossible to find. The complaint of a medical officer for the 11th Connecticut that he had received a thousand pillow cases and just a dozen sheets was echoed in various ways in almost every Northern regiment.

In the hope of imposing some order on this "chaos of benevolence," as Mary Livermore called it, the United States Sanitary Commission was born. The organization took its name from a British agency established during the Crimean War by the famed nurse Florence Nightingale to improve living conditions among the troops.

One of the American commission's founders was George Templeton Strong. It happened that the lower floor of the building in which Strong had his law offices was used to billet troops passing through New York on their way to the camps. Appalled by the filthy condition of the soldiers, Strong wrote in his diary: "I never knew before what rankness of stench can be emitted by unwashed humanity. It poisons the whole building and, of course, prevails in a concentrated form in the story they occupy, where its ammoniacal intensity is nauseous and choking. It half strangles me as I go upstairs." One trip up the stairs was enough to make him an impassioned advocate of better sanitation among the troops.

An even stronger advocate was Elizabeth Blackwell, the first woman trained as a physician in the United States. Dr. Blackwell called a meeting of 55 prominent New York women in late April of 1861 to plan the consolidation of all the aid societies recently established and to seek ways to cooperate with the U.S. Army Medical Bureau. But the bureau was cool to the idea, fearing that a civilian aid program would undermine military authority and conflict with the Army's own programs of treatment.

Nonetheless, Blackwell's group was able to enlist the support of an elite contingent of private doctors and other professional men and to carry the fight for recognition to Washington. There, Secretary of War Simon Cameron was petitioned to appoint a commission to consider the problems of squalor and disease among the troops.

On June 7, Cameron gave his grudging approval, although President Lincoln and his deputies were still frankly skeptical. To the President the commission looked like "a fifth wheel on the coach"—a gratuitous appendage to the Medical Bureau. A Cabinet member later confessed that "none of us had any faith in it," although the commission's work eventually converted them into believers.

For the key job of executive secretary the commission chose Frederick Law Olmsted, a talented administrator, writer and landscape architect who had supervised the design of New York's Central Park. Olmsted immediately set about enlisting the far-flung local aid societies, and put them to work under a central authority shipping supplies to designated depots.

At the same time, Olmsted organized a corps of sanitary inspectors and dispatched them to the Army camps. The campsites, they found, were filthy, fetid and poorly drained—ideal breeding grounds for dysentery, typhoid fever and other diseases. Food was stale and poorly cooked. Army physicians were scarce, overworked and powerless to cope with the miasmic conditions in the camps. A sanitary inspector in Illinois found pigs wallowing in a camp's water supply. Another inspector, in Virginia, asked a doctor if he needed more medicine for his typhoid patients. The physician replied no, because "the men die as a general rule anyhow."

To help hard-pressed Army doctors treat the sick and wounded, the commission's medical experts prepared booklets not only

Students of the Pennsylvania Academy of Fine Arts gather for a portrait with an enormous American flag that they stitched together in the spring of 1862 as a symbolic contribution to the Federal cause. Measuring 14 by 22 feet, the flag was displayed on the academy grounds

on camp cleanliness but on scurvy and dysentery, anesthesia and amputations. In addition, the commission left a permanent legacy in the form of statistical reports on "the physical, social, and moral condition of soldiers." Taken together, they constituted one of the most detailed analyses yet assembled of an army — so detailed, observed one commission member dryly, that "for general reading, I prefer Walter Scott."

Olmsted realized soon after taking over that the biggest obstacle to improving sanitation in the Army was the ossified leadership of the Medical Bureau. Equipped to serve a small professional force, the bureau had never administered a hospital of more than 40 beds. It was run by old men, observed the Reverend Henry W. Bellows, one of the commission's founders, and it carried on its business in a "style becoming a country apothecary."

With the aid of allies in Congress, the commission launched a shrewd campaign to force reorganization of the Medical Bureau. Members of the commission testified before the military committees of both houses of Congress and argued their case with the Secretary of War and the President himself. As a result of this pressure, the Surgeon General was replaced with a younger man, the Medical Corps was enlarged, and eight doctors were appointed to inspect sanitary conditions in the camps. The reorganization greatly improved relations between the Army and the Sanitary Commission — although later the commission faced sporadic resistance from Secretary Cameron's successor at the War Department, the irascible Edwin M. Stanton.

While Olmsted was fighting political battles in Washington, women volunteers at the commission's branches around the country were beginning to funnel civilian donations to the front. "The rush of business lasted all day and ran over into the midnight," recalled Mary Livermore, who had become director of the commission's Chicago office. In an article for a local newspaper, she described the hustle and bustle of a typical day there: "Early as is my arrival, a dray is already ahead of me, unloading its big boxes and little boxes,

Frederick Law Olmsted's vigorous direction of the U.S. Sanitary Commission turned it from a fledgling aid society into a national institution.

Sanitary Commission agents prepare to depart from Washington with a wagon full of supplies for the troops. Wrote one volunteer: "These hands of mine are hallowed by the hundreds of pairs of socks, the arm-slings, the crutches that they have been permitted to give to these heroes."

its barrels and firkins, baskets and bundles. In the receiving room, crammed boxes disgorge their contents, which are rapidly sorted, stamped, repacked and reshipped, their stay in the room barely exceeding a few hours. A bevy of nurses enter with carpet bags, shawls and bundles. They receive their instructions, commission, and transportation, and hurry onward. Soldiers from the city hospitals visit us to beg a shirt, a pair of slippers, a comb, or a well-filled pin cushion, something interesting to read, or paper, envelope and stamps." And all the while, she added, civilians would "come and go — to visit, to bring news from the hospitals, to make inquiries for missing men, to make donations of money, to retail their sorrows, and sometimes to idle away an hour in the midst of the hurrying, writing, copying, mailing, packing and shipping."

Many of the contributions that Livermore and the other volunteers distributed to the troops were accompanied by messages — simple, spontaneous expressions of affection. "My son is in the army," one note read. "Whoever is made warm by this quilt, let him remember his own mother's love." Other messages exhorted the soldiers to "keep up good courage" and not to "mope and have the blues." Some young women included their names and addresses and invited lonely soldiers to write to them. "When from war and camps you part," read one enclosed jingle, "may some fair knitter warm your heart!" Sometimes there was a reference to a specific action: "We send these supplies to the noble boys that beat back Bragg's army!"

All told, the commission distributed $15 million worth of stores to Federal soldiers in the field and in Confederate prison camps. The flow of goods diminished at times, as war weariness set in, but it never ceased entirely. In late 1863 the Confederates cut off the supply of goods to Union prisoners, in part because they observed that some of the boxes bore such labels as "For Our Starving Prisoners at Richmond." This interjection of propaganda into a humanitarian mission so incensed Confederate authorities that they maintained the ban for six months, lifting it only after the two governments had reached an agreement for mutual exchange of clothing and provisions.

The pressures of the War and the difficulties of obtaining transport eventually compelled the Sanitary Commission to play a much more active role in the field than it had originally intended. The only practical way to get large quantities of stores to the soldiers was to load them into wagons capable of following the armies wherever they moved. Accordingly, the commission began organizing its own wagon trains, known as "flying depots." This system enabled sanitary agents to reach the troops at Antietam with 30 barrels of bandages, more than 5,000 pounds of meat and 3,000 bottles of wine and liquor — then administered as tonic for the wounded. Commission wagons packed with blankets, woolen underwear and other goods followed the Army of the Potomac to Fredericksburg and then to Gettysburg.

To supplement the program of battlefield relief, the commission instituted a remarkable transport service to evacuate the sick and wounded from the war fronts and carry them to hospitals in the rear. Several steamers were obtained from the quartermaster general and fitted out as hospital ships; they were first used extensively in the Peninsular Campaign. Staffing them were doctors and nurses who had volunteered for the service.

On the recommendations of those in the field, the commission sought other ways to make the suffering of the wounded more bearable. Dr. Elisha Harris, a founding member, was appalled to see casualties of the Peninsular Campaign transported on the hard floors of rattling freight cars. He designed a hospital car in which litters were supported by rubber cords, enabling the patients to ride in relative comfort. Harris' cars were also equipped with operating tables and quarters for doctors and nurses.

Other members of the commission concentrated on disease control. When symptoms of scurvy began to appear in General Ulysses S. Grant's command in the Mississippi Valley in late 1862, the commission launched a campaign to collect potatoes and onions: Eaten raw, the two vegetables were known to cure scurvy. On the home front,

On a hospital train bound for Nashville in 1864, a Federal steward watches over his wounded charges — the jolting of their stretchers eased by bands of rubber. The special cars, designed by Dr. Elisha Harris of the U.S. Sanitary Commission, carried 225,000 patients during the War.

the commission staged talent shows that charged an admission fee of one potato or five onions. A widely reprinted "Letter from a Country Girl" urged all patriots to set aside a part of their gardens for the soldiers. "Don't send your sweetheart a love-letter," read a popular poster, "send him an onion." Soon as many as 1,000 barrels of vegetables and fruit were flowing each week into the camps of Grant's army.

The commission also established Soldiers' Homes as lodging for troops in transit, published a directory of the patients under treatment in every general hospital, and set up a claims office to help soldiers seeking pensions or back pay. When Union prisoners of war were released, the sanitary agents were often there to aid them.

The enormous variety of the commission's work gave it a wartime prestige that no other group possessed. Yet there were other aid organizations working both nationally and locally. Prominent among them were those that set up canteens at railway stations to provide hot meals for the vast numbers of troops on the move throughout the North. One of the busiest of these canteens was in Cleveland. There women started cooking,

A souvenir lithograph displays the bountiful services available to traveling soldiers at Philadelphia's Volunteer Refreshment Saloon. The establishment offered free bed and board; during the War its cooks dispensed more than 800,000 meals.

VOLUNTEER REFRESHMENT SALOON, SUPPORT

baking and brewing coffee as soon as they heard that a troop train was arriving — and repeated the process as often as necessary. At 4 p.m. on August 14, 1863, for example, volunteers were on hand to pass out hot food and coffee to the newly arrived veterans of the 4th Massachusetts. Four hours later, the women met and fed the 28th Maine, and at five the following morning they tendered the same greeting to the 47th Massachusetts.

Some canteens expanded their activities beyond the serving of food. The Union Volunteer Refreshment Saloon of Philadelphia, for example, offered dormitories, washrooms, a medical center, laundry service, and tables equipped with writing paper and stamps. The arriving soldier, wrote an eyewitness, "first performs his ablutions, then he eats his breakfast; after that he writes to his wife, and then he reads the news." Supported by local contributions, the Union Saloon cared for more than a half million men during the War.

Such services benefited the community as well. As the War progressed, civic leaders in the North became increasingly alarmed by the disorderly conduct of troops on leave or in transit. There were tavern fights, beatings and shootings involving troops in every major city. Trains between New York and Hartford were so jammed with drunken soldiers that women hesitated to make the trip even if accompanied. In this rowdy atmosphere, civilian canteens and refreshment saloons offered soldiers virtually the only alternatives to idle hours spent sitting in bars or roaming the streets.

Of all the women volunteers serving across the North, the nurses, the so-called "angels of the battlefield," were perceived as the real

...OUSLY BY THE CITIZENS OF PHILADELPHIA, PA.

heroines of the War. In fact, nursing in the war zones required women of extraordinary independence and determination. The prevailing opinion among soldiers and civilians at the start of the War was that women had no place in field hospitals. The less principled ones would flirt with the soldiers, the argument went, and all of them would be exposed to intimate and sordid details that no respectable women should see. So strong was this feeling that even the Sanitary Commission's own Henry Bellows asserted, "Women are rarely in place at the front, or even at the bases of the armies."

Women with the courage to volunteer for nursing were constantly harassed by Army doctors. An official Army report stated that females were best employed "in connection with extra diets, the linen-room and the laundry." Army surgeons, recalled nurse Sophronia Bucklin, engaged in "a systematic course of ill-treatment to drive women from the service." One doctor told Mary Livermore bluntly that if he had to tolerate women, he would rather it be the famously reticent Sisters of Charity, who "never write for newspapers, nor see or hear anything they shouldn't."

Against this wall of hostility several women battled with resounding success. One of the most formidable was a 59-year-old crusader from Massachusetts who rushed to Washington as soon as the War broke out. Dorothea Dix had gained a national reputation for her work in improving the treatment of the insane. Now she wanted to recruit a carefully selected corps of women nurses for the Army Medical Bureau. It was impossible, she was told — but she went ahead anyway. And when the Army finally agreed to accept an experimental nurses' corps, Dix was made its superintendent.

Her recruits worked for nothing at first. Later, Congress authorized payments of 40 cents a day, plus meals and transportation. Each of the women had to meet certain rigid standards established by Dix. They had to be "plain-looking," for one thing, and at least 30 years of age. Those given to jewels and other frivolities need not apply. "I am plain enough to suit you and old enough," one applicant wrote. "I have never had a husband and I am not looking for one. Will you take me?" She was accepted, along with 99 other volunteers. Some of the superintendent's recruits called her "Dragon Dix." But she prevailed, and gave the U.S. Army its first professional nursing corps.

Another pioneer in the field was Clara Barton. A 39-year-old schoolteacher in Massachusetts when war broke out, she was determined to have a part in the action. With the help of her close friend Henry Wilson, Chairman of the Senate Military Affairs Committee, she began to visit hospitals around Washington, handing out food and other supplies to wounded soldiers.

At first she paid out of her own pocket, but in time she was able to set up a network of contributors throughout New England. Churches, sewing circles and individuals sent donations; in return, she wrote them sprightly newsletters describing how the gifts were received by the soldiers.

In 1862, she decided to join the armies in the field. Her business, she explained, was "stanching blood and feeding fainting men," and her post was "the open field between the bullet and the hospital." By sheer tenacity, she wrangled permission from Surgeon General William A. Hammond to go to the front; the Army gave her a wagon for her stores.

Clara Barton soon won reknown for always being the first nurse to arrive on the battlefield. "I did not wait for reporters and journalists to tell us that a battle had been fought," she recalled afterward. "I went in while the battle raged." She was at her post on the night after the Second Battle of Bull Run, touring a hay-covered plain littered with fallen men, tending their wounds and ladling out coffee and water. "All night we made up compresses and slings," she wrote, "and bound up and wet wounds when we could get water and fed what we could in terror lest someone's candle fall into the hay and consume them all."

A few weeks later, at Antietam, she was raising the head of a wounded man to give him a drink when he was struck and killed by a Confederate bullet; the slug ripped a hole in her sleeve. Besides tending personally to the victims, she scavenged the area for food and whiskey to supplement her own supplies, doled out medicine and bandages to the doctors, and cooked up a batch of cornmeal gruel.

Clara Barton served through the War and became a legend — as did another fiercely independent nurse attached to the Union armies in the West. Mary Ann Bickerdyke, a 44-year-old widow from Ohio, first attracted attention by organizing the chaotic military hospital at Cairo, Illinois. Like the other great Army nurses, she was the special friend and protector of the common soldier — who responded by calling her "Mother Bickerdyke" and cheering her whenever she appeared. She meant more to the troops, an officer observed, "than the Madonna to Catholics."

When Grant's army moved down the Mississippi, Mother Bickerdyke went along to

Caring for Michigan's Own

Survivors of the savage fighting at Cold Harbor in the spring of 1864 cluster around the tents and soup kettles of the Michigan Soldiers' Relief Association at White House Landing in Virginia. Association agent Julia Wheelock (*seated, far left*) wrote of the suffering she saw there, "Were it not for the privilege of crying it seems my heart would break."

One of the more successful of the small, independent aid societies was the Michigan Soldiers' Relief Association, whose services were aimed exclusively at people of that state. From its Washington office, the association lent a helping hand to stranded soldiers, anxious relatives and bereaved families. It also dispatched women volunteers to seek out the sick, wounded and dying in nearby hospitals. One of these courageous agents was 29-year-old Julia S. Wheelock, who chronicled her missions of mercy in a personal journal.

Wheelock searched for soldiers from Michigan in the 15 hospitals of Alexandria, Virginia, and then provided food, clothing, blankets — and the comfort of a friendly voice. It was trying work, the more so since she lacked the official status enjoyed by agents of the Sanitary Commission and had to contend with indifference and even outright hostility on the part of military authorities. In time, she ventured to the Virginia battlefields to dispense lemonade, hot soup, gruel and tea to Michigan's walking wounded, and to do whatever was possible for the more seriously injured.

"O what scenes of suffering I have witnessed," she wrote in May of 1864 in a Fredericksburg hospital, while attending the wounded from the Spotsylvania Campaign. "In every hospital found many Michigan men without blankets, sometimes 50 or 60 in one room. Many who have just arrived from the front have had nothing to eat for three or four days — literally starving to death! Men were busy from early dawn until night burying the dead."

Two months later, after two years of "excessive labor, anxiety and excitement," Julia Wheelock contracted typhoid fever and was sent home to recuperate. She reported for duty again in Washington on April 13, 1865 — the day the capital celebrated the surrender of Lee's army at Appomattox.

set up one hospital after another with Sanitary Commission support. Convinced that the troops were not receiving enough dairy products, she once steamed up the Mississippi from Memphis to Illinois, cajoled farmers into contributing 200 milk cows and a thousand hens and organized a convoy to transport them back down the river. Her organizational skills were exceeded only by her energy. "She talks bad grammar," said a colleague, "jaws at us all, and is not afraid of anybody. But Lord, how she works!"

Stories about her independence delighted the Army. It was said, for example, that when an Army surgeon complained to General Sherman about Mother Bickerdyke's "insubordination," he was met with the reply: "If it was Bickerdyke, I can't do anything for you. She ranks me."

During four years of war, she went to the aid of the wounded on 19 battlefields. She was often the last person to leave the field at night, turning over bodies to make sure that no living had been left among the dead. Her last campaign was with Sherman in Georgia, and she marched with Sherman's veterans at the head of the ranks at war's end as they paraded past the White House.

Less flamboyant but equally dedicated were Georgeanna Woolsey and her married sister, Eliza Woolsey Howland. The two young women came from a cultured New York family: Their uncle Theodore was president of Yale College. Like many Northern families, the close-knit Woolsey clan was sundered by war. But in their case it was the women — Georgeanna and Eliza — who went off to the front first.

In the summer of 1861 they presented themselves as nursing candidates, an experience that Georgeanna said involved "taking the flowers out of my bonnet and the flounce off my dress, and toning up or toning down according to the emergency." As-

A field hospital set up by the United States Christian Commission at Gettysburg shelters men wounded in the battle there. When both armies moved out of Pennsylvania immediately after the fighting, the burden of caring for the 30,000 wounded left behind fell almost entirely on charitable organizations.

As his wife looks on, Dr. Gordon Winslow, a U.S. Sanitary Commission agent, enjoys a brief respite at the organization's Gettysburg headquarters. In the aftermath of the battle, the 59-year-old Winslow helped distribute more than 60 tons of food and myriad other items, including 10,000 shirts, 4,000 pairs of shoes and 110 barrels of bandage material.

signed to hospitals in Washington, they were at first harassed by surgeons who, according to Georgeanna, determined to make their lives "unbearable." But the sisters persevered, and when the Sanitary Commission fleet sailed for the Virginia Peninsula in 1862 the two Woolseys were aboard as members of the nursing staff.

The sisters moved from ship to ship as the thousands of men wounded in the Seven Days' Battles were taken aboard. Georgeanna feared that she was hardening. "We are changed by all this contact with terror," she wrote. The death of a man no longer shattered her: "I could not have quietly said, a year ago, 'That will make one more bed, doctor.'"

The family fretted about them. Their sister Jane, who did volunteer relief work at home, worried that they would exhaust themselves. She wrote them: "You will be wrung out and dried — yellow and gray." But the two persevered.

When the hospital ship *Daniel Webster* left the Peninsula, Eliza was the nurse-in-charge; her sister Georgeanna stayed behind with the army until it fell back toward Washington. Having arrived in New York, Eliza decided that she must give up professional nursing in order to take care of her husband, who had been discharged because of sickness. "I hate to be clean while you are dirty," she wrote apologetically to her sister. Georgeanna carried on — first at an Army hospital in Rhode Island and then at Gettysburg.

In a moving account written after the War, Georgeanna recalled her approach to the Gettysburg battlefield just after the fighting ended. She knew she was nearly there when she reached a barn where she saw a Confederate infantryman "sitting dead"; a pervading odor of decomposition hung in the air. In the torn landscape, she wrote, there was "no food, no rest, no cheer of any kind." A murky, warm rain began to fall, and through it came the wounded, limping and dragging themselves along.

The railroad bridges for miles around Gettysburg had been blown up, and relief trains were unable to get through. For three days, while the railroad was being repaired, Georgeanna Woolsey and a handful of other nurses cared for the shattered men in two hastily erected hospital tents. They washed and dressed wounds, handed out clean shirts and towels, served thousands of bowls of vegetable stew and glasses of milk spiked with whiskey. To ward off the stench coming off the battlefield, they prepared rags soaked in cologne.

After relief trains evacuated most of the wounded, the nurses continued to minister to the thousands of men who were too weak

to be moved. They gave food and shelter to any who needed it, Georgeanna wrote — "rebels and all." Of one Confederate lieutenant she recalled: "I could not think of him as a rebel; he was too near heaven for that." In three weeks on the field the nurses cared for 16,000 men. When the women finally left, Georgeanna Woolsey recalled proudly, they were escorted by two Army bands playing "Three Cheers for the Red, White and Blue."

The exploits of these and other heroic women were applauded in the press and repeated in homes throughout the North. But financial support for their efforts — and for other forms of war relief — became more difficult to find as the War itself became more costly. Fund raisers labored tirelessly to keep the cash flowing. "I have addressed large bodies and little bodies, and nobodies and somebodies," remarked one such volunteer for the Sanitary Commission. "I have spoken from pulpits and from judicial benches, before communion tables and baptismal fonts. I have seen before me eyes glistening with interest and eyes drowsy with sleep. I have heard stentorian yawns and rapturous applause."

By early 1862 contributions were so hard to come by that George Templeton Strong and the other leaders of the commission contemplated disbanding. What saved them for a time was an influx of money from the Far West — donations from the boom towns of California, which ultimately accounted for more than one fifth of the commission's income.

But even that was not sufficient. New money-making strategies were imperative. In Chicago, Mary Livermore, along with her colleague Jane Hoge, conceived the most spectacular Northern fund-raising institution of all: the sanitary fair.

The two women sent circulars to thousands of newspapers and churches in September 1863 announcing a "grand Northwestern fair" to be held in the city. The circular solicited articles to be sold or displayed for charity: knitwear and other homemade clothing, furniture and farm machinery, agricultural products, prepared foods, ornamental objects, flowers and wreaths, and "trophies, battle relics and mementoes of the war," including Confederate flags, sabers and "missiles of any kind." In addition, there would be a restaurant where prominent ladies would serve as hostesses, a nightly entertainment program, and dozens of other exhibits and attractions. The organizers hoped to net $25,000.

In came a flood of contributions. There were mowing machines and reapers, a howitzer, oil paintings and afghans and pianos, Durham bulls and toys and knitted drawers. Tracey G. Boon of Galesburg, Illinois, sent a "curious toothpick"; the workers of the Eagle Works Manufacturing Company of Chicago sent a steam engine.

The fair opened on October 27, 1863, with a three-mile-long parade through Chicago. Businesses, courts and schools shut down for the occasion. "By nine o'clock the city was in a roar," the Chicago *Tribune* reported. "The vast hum of multitudinous voices filled the atmosphere." A hundred farmers drove past in wagons decorated with flags and brimming with produce — "silver-skinned onions, mammoth squashes, barrels of cider and rosy apples." Soldiers and militiamen marched by with bands blaring. A row of wagons was filled with children singing

"John Brown's Body." A carriage containing several captured Confederate flags drew roars from patriotic spectators.

When the parade ended, the spectators surged into various exhibition buildings; for a 75-cent admission fee they could tour them all and get a meal as well. One hall was an art gallery, another displayed plows and heavy machinery, a third housed the battle trophies. Prominently featured for sale was the original draft of the Emancipation Proclamation. On donating it, President Lincoln had confessed to "some desire to retain the paper, but if it shall contribute to the relief or comfort of the soldiers, that will be better." The draft was bought at auction for $3,000 by one T. B. Bryan for the benefit of the Chicago Soldiers' Home.

The fair ran for a fortnight, with attendance averaging more than 5,000 a day. People flocked in from outlying areas as railroads offered discount tickets to fairgoers. When the organizers tallied the proceeds, they found that they had netted more than three times their goal.

Observing the success of the Chicago fair, a score of cities rushed to produce fairs of their own. All told, these efforts raised more than four million dollars to be channeled through agencies large and small for soldiers' relief. The fairs were, in a sense, the climax of this civilian campaign — a last, vast outpouring of benevolence.

The Sanitary Commission estimated that it raised and dispensed more than $25 million in aid during the War. The total from all sources came to at least $70 million.

Yet even this could not meet all needs — as volunteers working in the field were well aware. Many families of Union soldiers, for example, suffered grievously. No government insurance check or pension payment cushioned the blow when a soldier was killed, and if a man was taken prisoner his pay stopped until he rejoined his outfit. Early in the War, a Connecticut newspaper reported that auctioneers were helping soldiers' wives sell their furniture "where necessity compels the sacrifice." Two years later a war widow in Hartford and her two children were found weak and destitute, having eaten little more than a few potatoes in the preceding week. Nearly three fourths of the charity cases in Connecticut cities in the winter of 1864-1865 were military families. They were helped to some degree by local aid societies, and by trade associations and unions to which the soldiers had belonged. The police of New York, for example, set up the Metropolitan Police Fund for the relief of families of policemen who had gone to war. But such aid reached only a fraction of soldiers' families, leaving many in severe want.

Despite the shortcomings, the relief effort was amazingly comprehensive. And it greatly benefited morale on the home front by binding the populace in a common cause. An article in a Sanitary Commission newspaper declared that through such benevolence "neighbors and neighborhoods must come to respect each other more, to depend upon each other more, and wonder that they have missed finding each other out for so long."

Such was the lasting effect of civilian relief: It helped unify the Northern people. And the consensus that it kindled would be confirmed at the polls — thanks to the success of the Union armies and the political skills of President Lincoln.

Extravaganzas for Soldiers' Relief

The U.S. Sanitary Commission supported its vital relief work for the troops through popular fund-raising fairs that were part carnival and part Oriental bazaar. Known as sanitary fairs, these events were held in elaborately decorated halls in dozens of Northern cities. Altogether, they raised more than four million dollars. Ten thousand people a day paid admission to the largest fair of all, held in New York City in April 1864, to see a mélange of theatrical productions, Indian war dances and military displays.

At these fairs, a dizzying variety of items were offered for sale — everything from works of art to homemade jellies. At one fair a tame bear was auctioned off, at another a shipload of coal. Captured Confederate curiosities put on sale included a slave's shackle and a bell used on Jefferson Davis' plantation.

The phenomenal success of the fairs amazed even those who produced them. As a commission member wrote: "Who dreamed that the poor little Sanitary Commission would ever make such a noise in the world?"

A ticket to New York City's fair admitted the bearer to three restaurants, a multitude of shops, and galleries displaying fine arts and weaponry.

In a public square in Philadelphia near the Cathedral of St. Peter and Paul, the temporary buildings erected for the sanitary fair included a main pavilion flanked by a pair of rotundas. In all, the various galleries contained two miles of exhibits.

Posters seeking contributions to the restaurants at Philadelphia's fair stimulated an enormous outpouring of food and equipment. The fair's formidable main kitchen was manned by 30 cooks who produced thousands of meals a day.

GREAT CENTRAL FAIR

IN AID OF THE

SANITARY COMMISSION,

TO BE HELD AT
PHILADELPHIA,
FIRST WEEK IN JUNE, 1864

RESTAURANT
DEPARTMENT,

GEORGE T. LEWIS, CHAIRMAN.   MISS MARY McHENRY, CHAIRMAN LADIES' COMMITTEE

The Pennsylvania Kitchen,
MRS. H. P. M. BIRKINBINE, Chairman, 2221 Green Street.

The William Penn Parlor,
MISS ELLEN PRICE, Chairman, 38th and Chestnut Sts., West Philada.

Friends of the Sick and Wounded Soldiers, especially those residing in Pennsylvania, New Jersey and Delaware, make ready your Contributions for the support of this great and good work, let them be ever so small, they will be thankfully received.

Send by Railroad or Express: direct "For Restaurant Department, to care of A. R. McHenry, Chairman of Receiving Committee." Freight will be paid here.

Please put this up in a Conspicuous place.

Volunteer hostesses sell framed
works of art in a gallery at
New York's Metropolitan Fair.

A booth at the New York fair offer
variety of ornamental glassware.

Costumed Brooklyn women re-
create a Colonial-era kitchen in an
atelier of the Academy of Music.

manuel Leutze's painting of Washington crossing the Delaware dominates an exhibit at the New York fair.

Three attendants demonstrate a "self-sewer," an early sewing machine, at the Philadelphia fair.

A coconut palm, an exotic sight for New Yorkers, rises in the Grand Hall of the Metropolitan Fair.

Arms and uniforms surround a portrait of Colonel Elmer Ellsworth, the Union's first slain hero, in New York.

A myriad of exhibits in the vast central pavilion at Philadelphia's fair attracted droves of visitors, who contributed nearly a million dollars to the cause.

Fairgoers throng Brooklyn's Academy of Music during an 1864 sanitary fair. Trinkets made by Confederate prisoners proved popular novelties here.

The Political Battles

"The President has well maintained his position, and under trying circumstances acquitted himself in a manner that will be better appreciated in the future than now."

GIDEON WELLES, SECRETARY OF THE NAVY

5

"Party Politics! Party Politics!" wrote General in Chief Henry W. Halleck to a friend in 1863. "I sometimes fear they will utterly ruin the country."

Halleck was a choleric and suspicious man, but on the subject of wartime politics he was close to the mark. To many observers of the political battle, it sometimes seemed that the participants were more interested in attacking one another than in defeating the Confederacy.

Republicans and Democrats quarreled violently, not only across party lines but within their own ranks. Many of the Governors of the various states disputed the war powers claimed by the central government. And the firebrands in Congress denied Lincoln any presidential autonomy. "He is just as subject to our control as if we appointed him," declared Republican Senator Lyman Trumbull of Illinois. General Halleck was appalled to find that in Washington "*self,* and that little proud 'I' " seemed to rule the city. The politicians, he complained, "love the country some, but themselves a great deal more."

Moderates of both parties were disturbed to witness the growing polarization of politics. Every Federal defeat on the battlefield brought Radical Republican cries for "extirpation" of the Rebels and confiscation of their property. Among the so-called Peace Democrats, the cries were just as shrill for a policy of conciliation. Almost lost in the uproar were the voices of those moderate Republicans and War Democrats who supported Lincoln and his policies of gradual emancipation, persistence on the battlefronts and an equitable reconstruction.

To bring some order out of this factional chaos and forge a rough consensus, Lincoln drew on a range of political skills that astonished even his close associates. Artfully blending stubbornness and flexibility, persuasion and blunt force, he tirelessly pursued his overriding goal — the preservation of the Union. Yet his opponents in both parties were so tenacious that on the eve of his reelection bid in 1864 he expected defeat. The wonder is not just that he prevailed finally but that in the process he gave the riven North a sense of national purpose. He knew, as his friend T. J. Barnett of the Interior Department put it, that "the struggle within and without, with us, is for national existence" — and in the end, he managed to enlist the support of the Northern electorate in that struggle.

The first great political test of the Lincoln Administration came with the elections in the autumn of 1862. It was a bad time for the Republicans. Union armies were not performing well either in the East or the West. Prices and taxes were soaring. Farmers saddled with a glut of grain complained about shipping rates so high that they were virtually cut off from their markets. The draft, the suspension of habeas corpus, the fear of liberated black labor — all contributed to the

public gloom. Republican Senator James W. Grimes of Iowa was reflecting the sentiments of his constituency when he wrote angrily, "We are going to destruction as fast as imbecility, corruption, and the wheels of time can carry us."

In political circles, much of the resentment was directed against Lincoln. Many of the Governors were angry because he was so plainly taking power out of their hands: Already the federal government had assumed overall responsibility for recruitment. Such sins were compounded in the eyes of some state officials by Lincoln's apparent reluctance to use his power to abolish slavery.

In September of 1862 a group of 12 concerned Governors met in Altoona, Pennsylvania, to plot some common course of action — or as the fiery John A. Andrew of Massachusetts put it, to "save the President from the infamy of ruining the country." The Radical Republicans among them had the idea that they would withhold troops — which they had no legal right to do — unless Lincoln agreed to two conditions: first, to remove General George B. McClellan, a Democrat, as commander of the Army of the Potomac, and replace him with General John Frémont, a Republican and a staunch abolitionist; and second, to move to emancipate blacks and receive them into the Army.

As it turned out, the Governors made neither demand because Lincoln anticipated them. His Emancipation Proclamation was published even as they were meeting, thus depriving them of that issue. At the same time, Lincoln enlisted the support of the more moderate Governors at Altoona, such as David Tod of Ohio. Their influence helped restrain the extremists and blocked the movement in favor of Frémont. In the

end, the Governors meekly acknowledged that the President was their "responsible and constitutional head," and pledged him their "most loyal and cordial" support. But the extremists did not forget their grievances.

Also disgruntled as the elections approached were the Radical Republicans in Congress. Many were particularly angered in the summer of 1862 by Lincoln's open opposition to a highly punitive confiscation bill passed in both houses after bitter debate. It was the duty of the President, the bill declared, to seize all the property of specified classes of Southerners, or of any other persons who abetted the rebellion. The provision that Lincoln found most offensive was one calling for forfeiture of the property "extending beyond the lives of the guilty parties," so that their descendants could not inherit it. Such a provision, said Lincoln, was unconstitutional and vindictive.

He let it be known that he would veto the entire bill if the provision survived. Congress quickly passed a resolution that removed most of his objections, and Lincoln signed with misgivings. But he wanted his misgivings known: He sent his discarded veto message to the Congress, where it was read into the record amid the sneers and laughter of the Radicals.

The elections into which this badly splintered party entered in the autumn of 1862 involved governorships in six states and a large number of Congressional seats. The most important contest, the one for governor of New York, was marked by a bitter partisanship that was reflected in state after state.

As their nominee for governor, New York Democrats chose Horatio Seymour, a cultivated and articulate though chronically reluctant candidate who was prevailed upon to run by party leaders. Seymour was a wealthy lawyer and landowner who had served once before as governor, in the 1850s. He believed in a war to restore the Union but not to abolish slavery: The Constitution, he argued, guaranteed the protection of slavery by the states. As for the radical abolitionists, he pronounced them "animated by a vindictive piety, or a malignant philanthropy."

As it happened, Seymour's Republican opponent, James S. Wadsworth, was a fervent abolitionist who as military governor of Washington, D.C., had shown open contempt for the slaveholding population of that city. At every opportunity, Wadsworth had obstructed operation of the Fugitive Slave Law, refusing to return runaway slaves to their owners in the District.

Many of Seymour's rhetorical salvos during the campaign were directed at the Emancipation Proclamation, which Wadsworth passionately supported. In Seymour's view, the proclamation was an invitation to arson and murder by the freed slaves that would "invoke the interference of civilized Europe." Lincoln's suspension of habeas corpus elicited another Seymour blast. "Liberty is born in war," he cried, "it does not die in war." While he and his followers intended to support the Administration's war policy, Seymour maintained, they would resist any assault on civil liberties.

As the campaign heated up, partisans of both candidates abandoned all restraint. The editor of the New York *Herald,* James Gordon Bennett, wrote that if Wadsworth were elected, he would instigate a reign of terror unlike anything since the French Revolution. Not to be outdone, Henry Raymond of the New York *Times* insisted that a vote for Seymour was "a vote for treason."

Wadsworth proved more vulnerable than his opponent. His ardent abolitionism was much distrusted by New York's huge immigrant population, and his radical connections disturbed moderate Republicans. Seymour won by nearly 11,000 votes. Democrats also captured a majority of New York's Congressional seats.

Indeed, returns from around the North suggested that the voters were seriously dissatisfied with the state of the Union and the conduct of the War. Democrats prevailed in only two of the six gubernatorial races — Seymour in New York and Joel Parker in neighboring New Jersey — but the anti-Administration current flowed unmistakably through the Congressional elections. Five important states that had gone for Lincoln in 1860 — New York, Pennsylvania, Ohio, Indiana and the President's home state of Illinois — all sent a majority of Democrats to the House of Representatives. The Republicans increased their strength only in the border states.

By a narrow margin of 18 votes, the President's party remained the majority party in the House of Representatives. But the Republicans could take little comfort from the knowledge that some of the border state victories that preserved their Congressional majority were achieved at the point of Federal bayonets.

In Kentucky, for example, candidates were threatened with arrest if they ran on an anti-Administration platform. The military governor's office referred to the vote as a "kind of Military Census, telling how many loyal men there are in a county." In Missouri voters were required to take an oath of allegiance to the Union before they were admitted to the poll booths.

A crowd of people ravenous fo[r] news of the War gathers in Jun[e] 1862 outside the offices of the Pitt[s]burgh *Dispatch* to read a boar[d] summarizing the latest bulletins fro[m] the war fronts. Bad news from th[e] battlefields eroded the prestige [of] the Lincoln Administratio[n.]

Many complex issues had contributed to the erosion of Republican strength, including opposition to the Emancipation Proclamation, to new taxation and to conscription. But underlying everything else was simple weariness with the War. Republican George Templeton Strong had the impression that "we the people are impatient, dissatisfied, disgusted, disappointed." He compared the electorate to a feverish patient constantly shifting his position in bed "though he knows he'll be none the easier for it." The New York *Times* found the election a "vote of want of confidence" in Lincoln.

One lesson of the 1862 elections that no politician failed to heed was that the electorate was looking for simple answers to a crisis that was growing ever more complex. This trend encouraged the extremists of both parties. Following the shattering Union defeat at Fredericksburg, Radical Republicans in the Senate spearheaded a secret caucus of all the party's 32 Senators. They met on December 16, with the organizers determined to restructure the President's Cabinet and, as they saw it, save the nation.

The chief villain, in the Radicals' view, was Secretary of State William Seward. They thought — correctly — that Seward had more influence over Lincoln than any other Cabinet member, and they knew that his counsel was for moderation when they wanted more dramatic action. A few even suspected Seward of being a traitor. Thus Zachariah Chandler of Michigan wrote his wife that he believed Seward was "plotting for the dismemberment of the government." To Joseph Medill of the Chicago *Tribune* it was evident that Seward was "President *de facto*." He ruled the country, wrote Medill, by keeping "a sponge satura-

ted with chloroform at Uncle Abe's nose."

The caucus of Republican Senators passed a resolution calling for such changes in the Cabinet "as will secure to the country unity of purpose and action." This meant, explained Senator Orville Browning of Illinois, the removal of the moderate Seward faction and its replacement with "a cabinet of ultra men" whose leader would be Treasury Secretary Salmon P. Chase.

Chase was the only Cabinet member sufficiently radical to suit the Senators, and it was Chase who had spread stories about Seward's "back-stairs and malign influence" on Lincoln. Although he undoubtedly believed what he said about Seward, Chase's judgment was scarcely unclouded — for he and the Secretary of State were bitter rivals.

Chase was a man whose moral righteousness was so obtrusive that many people detested him. Ambitious, opinionated and convinced of his own rectitude, he had first made a name for himself as a lawyer by defending escaped slaves in Cincinnati against the claims of their owners. During six years in the Senate and two terms as governor of Ohio, he confirmed his promise as one of the most vigorous of the antislavery political leaders. Lincoln, after watching Chase's prodigious — and largely effective — labors as Secretary of the Treasury, concluded that he was "about one and a half times bigger than any other man I ever knew."

Seward shared Chase's dislike of slavery, but not his intransigence or his pomposity. Having entered politics as a firebrand abolitionist — first as governor of New York and later as senator — Seward gradually modified his views and became a voice of restraint in both domestic and foreign affairs. To Chase, this proved that Seward was a blatant opportunist. Moreover, Chase could not abide Seward's style. Seward was as witty as Chase was humorless: At his house on Lafayette Square, the Secretary of State presided over one of the liveliest tables in Washington. To a man who thought it was a sin to waste time, such sociability betokened a lack of seriousness. "I have never been able to establish much sympathy between us," wrote Chase dourly of his relationship with Seward.

The Radical Republican Senators who looked to Chase for leadership decided to appoint a nine-man deputation to call on the President and present their views. When Lincoln received them, Senator Jacob Collamer of Vermont read a statement demanding that the President appoint a Cabinet of men wholly committed to the War. Various Senators then attacked Seward, depicting him as a negative influence in the Cabinet, and a man who preferred a negotiated peace to a clear-cut military victory. Lincoln defended his Secretary of State and his Cabinet vigorously. But he was too shrewd a politician to reject the Cabinet reorganization plan outright. He told the Senators he would consider it.

In fact, Seward had already heard of the charges being made against him, and had submitted his resignation. After failing to get him to change his mind, Lincoln put the resignation aside for the moment and called his Cabinet into session, without Seward. He explained in detail the accusations that were being made. Then he asked the Cabinet members to reconvene with him that night, when he was scheduled to have his next meeting with the dissident Senators.

It was a clever political move. The eight Senators present at the second conference lost some of their assurance when confronted with the Cabinet, again minus Seward. At the same time, Chase was put in the awkward position of being asked to spell out openly the case against Seward. Instead of doing so, he made a vague and vacillating statement that alienated both the Senators and the other Cabinet members. Near the end of the meeting, Lincoln asked the Senators present if they still wanted Seward's resignation. Four said yes, but the other four refused to commit themselves. The Senators then withdrew in some confusion, saying that they needed time to reflect.

Lincoln moved resolutely after that, sending for Chase and telling him that he was seriously disturbed about the veiled criticisms of Seward made before the Senators. As he expected, Chase tendered his resignation. "Now I can ride," Lincoln exulted. "I have got a pumpkin in each end of my bag."

Lincoln let the Radicals know that if Seward was to leave the Cabinet, Chase would have to go too. Then he wrote to both Seward and Chase, asking them to withdraw their resignations. "The trouble is ended," Lincoln said, and he was right. The Radicals would continue to oppose him, but there was never again Senatorial talk of trying to reorganize the Cabinet — or go over the President's head.

In this, as in other political crises, Lincoln revealed his consummate flexibility. He knew what he wanted to achieve, but he bided his time until he saw how the opposing interests could be made to work for him. He was particularly attentive to the political scene in the first months of 1863 — for the parties were in a state of flux.

It was a period of frustration for the Union armies. And to proponents of states' rights, it seemed that the federal government was

Treasury Secretary Salmon P. Chase, a favorite of the Radical Republicans, stands at left as President Lincoln reads the Emancipation Proclamation to his Cabinet. Secretary of State William H. Seward, a moderate whom Chase tried to discredit, sits with his legs crossed at right.

intent on crushing the last vestiges of local freedom and initiative. Conscription, arbitrary arrests, heavy taxation, federal meddling in state and local elections — all were bitterly criticized and sometimes resisted.

As elections approached in the spring of 1863, the Copperhead Democrats became steadily shriller in their denunciations of the War, the draft and emancipation. The only way for the country to know peace, they suggested, was through a political revolution. While the Republicans could count on Lincoln to keep the Radicals in check, the Democrats had no way of curbing their own extremists. And as the rhetoric of the Copperheads veered toward defeatism and outright disloyalty, War Democrats fled the party. In some places they voted straight Republican; in others they joined forces with Republicans to form a coalition known as the Union Party.

In the spring elections, the Republicans and their Union Party allies made important gains from New England to the Midwestern farm belt. They took control of the legislature in New Hampshire and won the governorship there, carried judicial and local elections in Michigan and Ohio, and severely cut Democratic strength in former Copperhead strongholds in Indiana, Iowa and Missouri. Despite these results, however, Ohio Democrats persisted in nominating the most famous Copperhead of all, the exiled Clement Vallandigham, as candidate for governor that fall.

In doing so, they ignored the fact that Vallandigham could not reenter the Union on pain of arrest. Throughout the campaign he remained on the Canadian side of Niagara Falls, making his views known through his faithful disciples.

Secretary Chase's Designing Daughter

In the eyes of many, the most accomplished hostess in wartime Washington was Kate Chase (*right*), the beautiful young daughter of Treasury Secretary Salmon Chase. She was arguably the most ambitious as well. Like her father, who long coveted the presidency, she wanted badly to live in the White House.

Described by an observer as "tall and slender, and exceedingly well formed," Kate Chase arrived in the capital from her native Ohio in 1861 at the age of 20. She was soon hosting parties for her widower father, beaming her considerable charms on anyone who could help Chase gain the 1864 Republican nomination. To help finance her endeavor, Kate married William Sprague IV, a Rhode Island politician and textile manufacturer, said to be worth $25 million.

Despite Kate's efforts, her father's presidential designs were thwarted. After he died in 1873, her life began to unravel. Sprague, who had proved a drunken philanderer, lost his fortune, and Kate was linked in scandal with New York Senator Roscoe Conkling. Before her death in 1899, she had fallen into poverty, subsisting by raising chickens and vegetables and peddling them door to door.

A formal portrait shows Kate Chase and William Sprague shortly after their ill-fated marriage in 1863.

If anything, exile had sharpened Vallandigham's tongue. He attacked the Emancipation Proclamation as unconstitutional and abolitionists as traitors. He urged negotiations with the Confederacy, and insinuated that Lincoln's war had no other objective than to liberate the blacks and enslave the whites. George Pugh, Vallandigham's running mate, counseled Ohioans to vote for Vallandigham or "sell your goods and chattels and emigrate to some other country, where you can find freedom."

Here as elsewhere, such rhetoric played into the hands of the Copperheads' opponents. Ohio Republicans banded together with disenchanted War Democrats to oppose Vallandigham under the banner of the Union Party. They put up John Brough, a former state auditor and president of the Madison & Indianapolis Railroad, who declared himself solidly behind Lincoln and the War. Both sides traded gratuitous insults (Vallandigham was derided for neglecting his widowed mother and Brough for being grotesquely fat) and both sides accused the other of virtual treason. In

Vallandigham's hometown of Dayton, one Democrat and one Republican were shot to death in political arguments.

Taking no chances, Lincoln granted furloughs to Ohio troops, and authorized 15-day leaves for federal clerks from Ohio, so they could go home and vote. He need not have worried: Brough won in a landslide. Lincoln got the news in the War Department's telegraph office, where he was spending an anxious night. "Glory to God in the highest," he reportedly wired Brough. "Ohio has saved the nation."

In fact, moderate Republicans and their War Democrat allies captured every important election that fall. Pennsylvanians reelected Governor Andrew Curtin over a Peace Democrat candidate supported by General George McClellan. Other Republican Governors were returned to office in Iowa, Massachusetts, Maine and Wisconsin. Even in Maryland, voters chose Union Party candidates in four of the five Congressional races. Politicians read the 1863 returns as a decisive repudiation of the movement for a compromise peace. "The people have voted in favor of the war," one disheartened Copperhead lamented.

As 1864 began, Lincoln seemed in a fairly strong position to win reelection to the presidency. The Peace Democrats had been temporarily silenced, and personal attacks on the President had subsided. But Lincoln knew as well as anyone that the wartime electorate was highly volatile. He also realized that within his own party there was strong sentiment against granting him a second term.

Behind this was a popular notion that no President should occupy the office for more than one term: The last President to do so had been Andrew Jackson. And there was lingering doubt among Republicans that Lincoln was up to the job. Even people who knew him mistook his patient, judicious style for indecisiveness and vacillation. If his secretary John Hay could extol him for being "so wise, so gentle, and so firm," others like the Reverend Henry Ward Beecher found him lacking the "element of leadership." Lincoln's mind, added Beecher, "works in the right directions, but seldom works clearly and cleanly."

Opposition to the President from Radical Republicans had erupted anew after he delivered his annual message to Congress on December 8, 1863. It was a fairly routine address until its last paragraphs, in which Lincoln laid out his ideas for a postwar South. In essence, his plan called for a full pardon for most of the Southern population and the restoration of state governments with the same rights and privileges they had enjoyed before the War.

Nothing, wrote William Cullen Bryant in the New York *Evening Post,* "could be more magnanimous." Moderate Republicans rejoiced, in the words of John Hay, "as if the millennium had come." Lincoln was acclaimed for having produced a document that was at once statesmanlike and humane.

But many Radical Republicans were furious. The defeated South must remain subjugated, they said, until all vestiges of rebellion had been rooted out. By their acts of secession the states had ceased to exist Constitutionally, and the federal government would be making a grave mistake to reconstitute them as they had been before. "The whole broad Rebel region is *tabula rasa,* or a clean slate," declared Massachusetts Senator Charles Sumner. Pennsylvania Congressman Thaddeus Stevens thundered: "The foundations of Southern institutions must be broken up and relaid, or all our blood and treasure have been spent in vain." The implication was clear: The South should be carved into new political entities as one of the penalties of rebellion.

Radicals holding these views soon set up a national committee, with Senator Samuel Clarke Pomeroy of Kansas as its nominal head, to campaign for Treasury Secretary Salmon Chase as the Republican presidential candidate. Whether Chase knew about their efforts in advance is unclear, but he was on record as saying that "a man of different qualities from those the President has will be needed for the next four years."

In a written statement soon known as the Pomeroy Circular, the committee argued that the reelection of Lincoln was "practically impossible," that his incumbency was damaging to "the cause of human liberty and the dignity and honor of the nation," and that Chase was the only man who could retrieve the situation. By accident or design, the letter was published in the press; it provoked a different response than its authors expected. The document unleashed a flood of support for Lincoln. Abetted by key Administration supporters, the legislators of state after state passed resolutions in favor of the President's reelection. Even in Chase's home state of Ohio, the legislature came out for Lincoln. The Treasury Secretary lamely apologized to his chief, withdrew his name from the presidential contest, and the Pomeroy rebellion was over. It had proved "more dangerous in its recoil," observed Navy Secretary Gideon Welles dryly, "than in its projectile."

But the effort to dump Lincoln was not quite dead. At the end of May a small band

After being relieved from two military commands during the War, General John C. Frémont emerged as the presidential candidate of a short-lived anti-Lincoln party in 1864. After the War, Frémont engaged in dubious railroad-building schemes and was eventually convicted of fraud.

of Radical Republicans held a convention in Cleveland to choose their own candidate. They selected John Frémont, the prominent explorer who had been the Republican Party's first presidential nominee eight years earlier. In 1861 Frémont had been removed by Lincoln as commander of Union forces in Missouri after issuing his own proclamation emancipating the slaves of all persons in that state who resisted the federal government.

Frémont, who still harbored bitter feelings toward Lincoln, proclaimed that the country was suffering from "the abuses of a military dictation without its unity of action and vigor of execution." The quixotic hope of Frémont's tiny splinter party was to form an alliance with disgruntled Republicans of all stripes to deny Lincoln the nomination. Some of Lincoln's advisers feared the same thing, but the President remained calm.

In fact, Lincoln had a virtual stranglehold on the Republican Party — which called itself the National Union Party during the campaign to attract Democrats. Lincoln's managers not only controlled the party machinery but also the disposal of patronage jobs across the country — provost marshals, postmasters, federal posts of all descriptions — and the awarding of contracts. When the National Union convention met in Baltimore in early June, virtually every state delegation had been instructed to vote for Lincoln. Judge David Davis, one of Lincoln's old political allies in Illinois, declined to travel to Baltimore, saying he knew the outcome in advance.

As it turned out, the recalcitrant Missouri delegation cast its 22 votes for General Ulysses S. Grant amid what one witness described as "growls of disapproval." Other-wise, the polling went as expected. With the final tally at 484 to 22, the Missourians reversed their vote to make it unanimous.

Lincoln learned of his renomination in the War Department telegraph room. To broaden the ticket's appeal, the convention had nominated for vice president War Democrat Andrew Johnson, the Governor of occupied Tennessee. "Send the telegram right over to the madam," Lincoln said. "She will be more interested than I am." He was under no illusions about his renomination. The convention, he said, had not judged him "either the greatest or the best man in America," but had simply concluded not "to swap horses while crossing the river."

His popularity was, in fact, firmly established and growing. The view of many moderate politicians was expressed by Illinois Congressman Owen Lovejoy: "If he is not the best conceivable President, he is the best possible." The poet and editor William Cullen Bryant wrote that he was "popular with the plain people, who believe him honest, with the rich people, who believe him safe, with the soldiers, who believe him their friend, and with religious people, who believe him to have been specially raised up for this crisis."

But Lincoln himself knew that he did not really control the crisis; he admitted that inevitably "events have controlled me." Now, in the hot summer of this election year, events conspired to cast a heavy cloud of gloom over the Republicans. Grant near Petersburg and Sherman before Atlanta were both stalled; Jubal Early's Confederate raiders swept to the outskirts of Washington; the President was forced to call for a half million more recruits; and the price of gold soared to new highs. Horace Greeley wrote in July that "the business of the country is all but fatally deranged."

The prestige of the Administration plummeted, and the country was now witness to an extraordinary spectacle—factions of the Republican Party trying to replace the President they had just renominated. Not a month after the convention, Lincoln found himself in an open rupture with Salmon Chase. The Secretary had used his influence to try to get one of his supporters appointed assistant treasurer at the branch of the U.S. Treasury in New York. Lincoln objected, fearing that the appointment would alienate New York moderates whose support he needed. The fiery Chase once again submitted his resignation, and this time Lincoln accepted. He wrote to Chase on June 30: "You and I have reached a point of mutual embarrassment in our official relation which it seems can not be overcome."

Chase's resignation unleashed a storm of anti-Lincoln rhetoric in the Senate, with the Radicals renewing their attacks on Lincoln's reconstruction plan for the South. Their offensive took the form of a severe and vengeful reconstruction bill pressed through the Senate by Ohio Senator Ben Wade and through the House by Maryland Representative Henry Winter Davis. Lincoln refused to sign it, citing several objections. One of the most important was that the bill assumed the Confederate states to be outside the Union, thus implying that states could dissolve their connection with the Union when they wished. Neither the federal government nor the concept of nationhood, Lincoln said, could "survive that admission. If it be true, I am not President and these gentlemen are not Congress."

Congressman Davis reacted to the pocket

An unusual photograph of George B. McClellan, probably taken when he was running for President, shows the general wearing civilian clothes rather than his accustomed uniform. The Democrats' hope that McClellan's military fame would help him defeat Lincoln was reflected in a campaign song of the time: "O General McClellan, he is the man / He licked the Rebels at Antietam."

veto by predicting civil war in the North unless Republicans reversed their convention vote and rejected Lincoln. Davis then issued a searing indictment that accused the President of "dictatorial usurpation." Colleagues of Davis sent out a call for Republican Party leaders to meet in September to discuss the withdrawal of Lincoln's nomination and to "concentrate the Union strength on a candidate who commands the confidence of the country." The mercurial Horace Greeley took up the cry: "Mr. Lincoln is already beaten; he cannot be elected and we must have another ticket." New York political boss Thurlow Weed told the President the same thing to his face. Abolitionist agitator John Jay proposed that Lincoln write a letter renouncing his nomination.

Lincoln remained determined. As the

Democratic convention approached in late August, he predicted that his opponent would be either "a Peace Democrat on a war platform, or a War Democrat on a peace platform." It turned out to be the latter, in the person of George B. McClellan, whom Lincoln had removed from his Army command in the fall of 1862. A year later, McClellan had made known his opposition to the President by endorsing a Democrat for governor of Pennsylvania. After that, he circulated the word quietly that he was available as a candidate for the presidency.

Chicago gamblers were offering 4-to-1 odds in favor of McClellan as Democrats streamed into Chicago for the convention that opened August 29. Fractious as ever, the Democrats were split between McClellan men, who favored a military victory to restore the Union, and peace advocates, who favored an armistice and negotiation.

The peace contingent was strong enough to demand a compromise: They would accept McClellan's nomination if they could write the platform. Clement Vallandigham, who had returned defiantly from Canada only to be ignored by the government, was one of the principal authors of that document. Its key section denounced "four years of failure to restore the union by the experiment of war" and demanded "immediate efforts for a cessation of hostilities with a view to an ultimate convention of all the states." The platform stopped short of approving secession and remained silent on the subject of slavery. Although it pleased neither the Peace Democrats nor the War Democrats, this compromise was passed with only four dissenting votes. The convention then sealed the bargain by nominating McClellan, who at once repudiated the peace plank.

Just five days later, Northerners read in

In an 1864 cartoon, General McClellan tries to whitewash the party's peace platform as his running mate, George H. Pendleton, looks on angrily (left) and Democratic leaders shout objections (right). McClellan repudiated the Democrats' call for an immediate peace with the Confederacy, saying that "the Union must be preserved at all hazards."

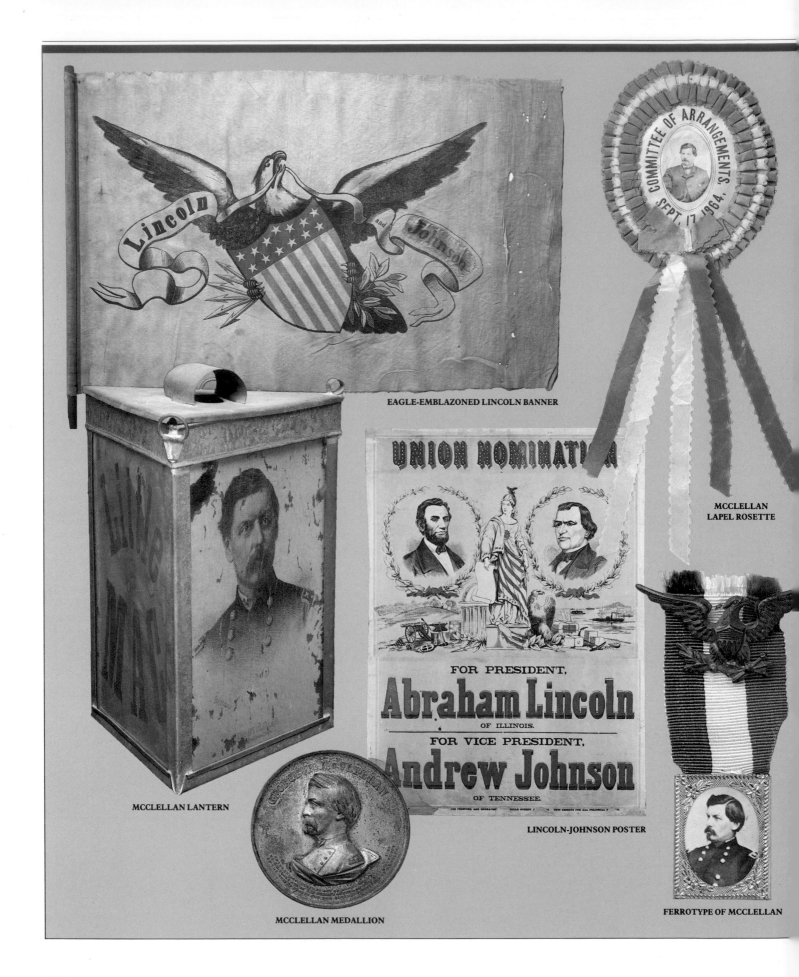

EAGLE-EMBLAZONED LINCOLN BANNER

MCCLELLAN
LAPEL ROSETTE

COMMITTEE OF ARRANGEMENTS.
SEPT. 17 1964.

MCCLELLAN LANTERN

UNION NOMINATION

FOR PRESIDENT,
Abraham Lincoln
OF ILLINOIS.
FOR VICE PRESIDENT,
Andrew Johnson
OF TENNESSEE.

LINCOLN-JOHNSON POSTER

MCCLELLAN MEDALLION

FERROTYPE OF MCCLELLAN

Campaign Paraphernalia from a Presidential Race

Nineteenth Century presidential campaigns brought forth a dazzling variety of political souvenirs, and the Lincoln-McClellan contest was no exception. Private mints struck coinlike medallions of the candidates. Textile houses produced everything from banners to bookmarks blazoned with pictures of the nominees or with patriotic symbols. Posters proliferated, as did examples of the young art of photography — small ferrotypes of the candidates mounted as lapel decorations. Most interesting of all were campaign lanterns, many of them three-sided kerosene lamps with the candidates' names and likenesses printed on their glass panels. These lanterns were carried during the riotous torchlight processions that snaked their way through the towns and cities of the Union.

LINCOLN CLOTH BOOKMARK

Published by Cha⁵ Magnus, 12 Frankfort St. N.Y.

HAIL TO THE NOMINEE.

All hail! Unfurl the stripes and stars!
The banner of the free!
Ten times ten thousand patriots greet
The shrine of Liberty;
Come, with one heart, one hope, one aim,
An undivided band,
To elevate, with solemn rites,
The ruler of our land.

Not to invest a potentate
With robes of majesty—
Not to confer a kingly crown,
Nor bend a supple knee,
We bow beneath no scepter'd sway,
Obey no royal nod—
Columbia's sons, erect and free,
Kneel only to their God!

Our ruler boasts no titled rank,
No ancient, princely line—
No legal right to sovereignty,
Ancestral and divine.
A patriot, at his country's call,
Responding to her voice—
One of the people, he becomes
A sovereign by our choice.

And now before the mighty pile
We've rear'd for Liberty,
He swears to cherish and defend
The charter of the free!
God of our country! seal his oath
And let him be awake,
God save the Union of the States
God save "our little Mac."

THE UNION FOREVER.

FOR PRESIDENT
Abraham Lincoln.
FOR VICE PRESIDENT
Andrew Johnson.
FOR PEACE COMMISSIONERS
GRANT & SHERMAN.

LINCOLN-JOHNSON BOOKMARK

GRAND RALLY
McCLELLAN
THE UNION & THE CONSTITUTION!
R PRESIDENT OF THE UNITED STATES

EORGE B. McCLELLAN

GRAND MASS MEETING
To Ratify our Nominations for President and Vice President, will be held

N THE PARK!
In front of the Methodist Church, Derby, Conn.,

ATURDAY EV'G, SEPT. 3, at 8 o'clock.

N. A. C. DAVIS,   HON. GEO. W. STEVENS.

A Salute of THIRTY FOUR GUns, in honor of the Nominations, will announce the Commencement of the Meeting.
Per order of Committee of Arrangements.

BAPTIST & TAYLOR, Steam Book and Job Printing Building, cor. Fulton and Nassau Streets, N.Y.

POSTER ADVERTISING A McCLELLAN RALLY

**LINCOLN-JOHNSON
CAMPAIGN LANTERN**

their morning papers the news that would turn the election campaign upside down: Sherman had at last taken Atlanta. George Templeton Strong hailed it as "the greatest event of the war." Coupled with Admiral Farragut's success in Mobile Bay a few weeks earlier, Sherman's breakthrough gave the wavering, war-weary Yankees the infusion of confidence they so urgently needed. Church bells rang out in village squares across the North.

Republicans who had been ready to jettison Lincoln two weeks earlier now hastened to fall in line behind him. The proposed meeting to choose another candidate was cancelled. The President seized the advantage. He solicited the support of such powerful editors as Horace Greeley and James Gordon Bennett by dangling high level posts before them — postmaster general for Greeley and ambassador to France for Bennett. Greeley forgot his premature dismissal of the President's chances and declared that "we must reelect him, and, God helping us, we will." At the end of September, Frémont reluctantly withdrew as a candidate in the interest of party unity.

Now the Democrats' position was obviously very difficult: How could they go before the public asserting the War's failure when every week brought fresh news of success? At the same time, they were wary of making major issues of either emancipation or reconstruction for fear of further splitting their own party.

Lacking substantive issues, they resorted to personal attacks. Lincoln was smeared as a "filthy story-teller," a thief, and "ignoramus Abe." But the insults had little effect on the voters' trust in Lincoln. He was strongly supported by skilled workers

For voting in the field, some Federal regiments employed ballot boxes such as the one shown here. To cast his vote, a soldier selected either a white ball or a black cube from the front of the box, then slipped the token through a hole into the rear compartment. After a number of votes had been cast, an officer opened the hinged lid to count the results.

and professional people in the cities — who were faring well in the wartime economy — and his popularity among rural folk was unassailable. The correspondent of the London *Daily News* observed that country people were attracted rather than repelled by his awkwardness of dress and sometimes of manner: "His logic and his English, his jokes, his plain common sense, his shrewdness, his unbounded reliance on their honesty and straight-forwardness, go right to their hearts."

As the campaign heated up, thousands of rallies were held across the land for both candidates. An avid Lincoln supporter remembered: "Night and day, without cessation, young men like myself, in halls, upon street corners and from cart tails, were haranguing, pleading, sermonizing, orating and extolling our cause and our candidate, and denouncing our opponents."

For all the signs favoring the Administration, Lincoln was uneasy and taking no chances. Statewide elections were coming up on October 11 in Ohio, Indiana and Pennsylvania, and the President granted thousands of presumably pro-Union soldiers furloughs to go home and vote. He wrote personally to Sherman suggesting that all of Indiana's soldiers, "or any part of them, go home to vote at the state election." Sherman understood the suggestion as a command. By an administrative error, the men of the 19th Vermont Volunteers were among the troops sent to Indiana, and they were allowed to vote there, although many of the state's qualified Democratic voters were challenged at the polls.

After Administration supporters swept all three of the state contests, Lincoln remarked the slightest of margins: Calculating on the back of a blank telegraph form, he figured he would take the election by 117 electoral votes to 114 for McClellan.

In the final days before the election, the northbound trains out of Washington were jammed with soldiers and government workers going home to vote. Convalescent soldiers were released from hospitals to go to the polls. Some states allowed their soldiers

In a sketch by artist William Waud, Pennsylvania troops line up to cast paper ballots near the headquarters of the Army of the James, part of the force that was besieging Petersburg in 1864. Even the units that had suffered heavy losses supported Lincoln's war policies, one corps returning 5,176 votes for Lincoln versus 2,079 for McClellan.

to a friend, "It does look as if the people wanted me to stay here a little longer." But he relaxed none of his efforts in the presidential campaign. He went so far as to order government employees to support the National Union Party ticket or lose their jobs. Troops, howitzers and ambulances full of wounded men were paraded through Washington in patriotic torchlight processions. Such measures reflected Lincoln's apprehension that the contest might be decided by

to vote in the field, although the balloting was scarcely fair. Colonel Theodore Lyman, serving in General George Meade's command, saw a fellow officer who talked in favor of McClellan mustered abruptly out of the service. "You would scarcely credit the number of such cases as this," he wrote.

There was considerable evidence of ballot-tampering at post offices and elsewhere—with soldiers' Democratic ballots being replaced with National Union ones. In some

Standing beside a small iron table and surrounded by notables on the Capitol steps, Lincoln reads his second inaugural address on March 4, 1865. Many in the throng at the ceremony were moved to tears by the speech's most memorable line: "With malice toward none; with charity for all."

regiments, soldiers who wanted to vote for McClellan found that there were simply no Democratic ballots available.

On the evening of election day, November 8, President Lincoln took up the vigil at the War Department telegraph office. The first good news came from Indianapolis, then Baltimore and Massachusetts. New York reported a narrow win for Lincoln. By midnight he was certain of victory: Pennsylvania, all of New England, Ohio, Indiana, Michigan and Maryland were his. An hour later he added his home state of Illinois to the list. Lincoln stepped outside to acknowledge a crowd of jubilant serenaders. "I give thanks to the Almighty," he told them, "for this evidence of the people's resolution to stand by free government and the rights of humanity."

The complete returns gave Lincoln 55 per cent of the popular vote and the electoral votes of every state but New Jersey, Kentucky and Delaware, for a total of 212 to 21. Without the soldiers' vote — which went 4 to 1 for Lincoln — the contest would have been much closer. But as it was, the President's sweeping victory helped to increase Republican majorities in Congress. "The most momentous popular election ever held since ballots were invented," George Templeton Strong declared with partisan fervor, "has decided against disunion."

In fact, that decision had already been made, when both candidates committed themselves to winning the War and restoring the rebellious states to the Union. In that sense the election simply confirmed the painful emergence of nationhood out of the turmoil of conflicting interests dividing the North.

The Faces of Lincoln

"There are many pictures of Lincoln, there is no portrait of him." So wrote the President's secretary John Nicolay. He added: "The picture was to the man as the grain of sand to the mountain, as the dead to the living. Graphic art was powerless before a face that moved through a thousand delicate gradations." For many photographers, that face was an endlessly fascinating challenge. About 120 photographs of Lincoln survive; shown here are 10 that span the years of his presidency.

FEBRUARY 9, 1861

CIRCA 1862

APRIL 17, 1863

AUGUST 9, 1863

NOVEMBER 8, 1863

CIRCA 1864

1863 OR 1864

WITH SON TAD, FEBRUARY 9, 1864

FEBRUARY 1864

MARCH 1865

ACKNOWLEDGMENTS

The editors wish to thank the following individuals and institutions for their valuable assistance in the preparation of this volume:

Indiana: Indianapolis — Carolyn Autry, Indiana Historical Society Library.

Nebraska: Lincoln — John Carter, Nebraska State Historical Society.

New York: Philip B. Kunhardt Jr., New York City — Thomas P. Davis, Renée Klish, James Mellon.

Pennsylvania: Carlisle — Randy Hackenburg, Michael J. Winey, U.S. Army Military History Institute. Harrisburg — Richard A. Sauers, Pennsylvania Capitol Preservation Committee. Philadelphia — Russ Pritchard, War Library and Museum of the Military Order of the Loyal Legion of the United States. Pittsburgh — Mary Ellen McBride. Swedes Ford — William Oliver. Upper Darby — J. Craig Nannos.

Virginia: Alexandria — Susan Cumbey, Wanda Dowell, Fort Ward Museum and Park. Falls Church — Chris Nelson.

Washington, D.C.: Austin R. Lawrence, Heritage Gallery; Scott W. Baker, Moorland-Spingarn Research Center, Howard University; Eveline Nave, Photoduplication Service, Library of Congress; Barbara Burger, Deborah Edge and Staff, Still Pictures Branch, National Archives; Larry Bird, Vanessa Broussard, Joyce Lancaster, Lorene Mayo, Anne Serio, L. W. Vosloh, National Museum of American History, Smithsonian Institution; Wayne D. Rasmussen, U.S. Department of Agriculture; John Childers, U.S. Senate Rules Committee.

The index for this book was prepared by Nicholas J. Anthony.

BIBLIOGRAPHY

Books

Bacon, Georgeanna M., *Letters of a Family during the War for the Union, 1861-1865*. Privately printed, no date.

Baker, Nina Brown, *Cyclone in Calico: The Story of Mary Ann Bickerdyke*. Boston: Little, Brown, 1952.

Barton, William E., *The Life of Clara Barton: Founder of the American Red Cross*. 2 vols. Boston: Houghton Mifflin, 1922.

Basler, Roy P., ed., *The Collected Works of Abraham Lincoln*. Vols. 5 and 7. New Brunswick, N.J.: Rutgers University Press, 1953.

Berlin, Ira, ed., *Freedom: A Documentary History of Emancipation, 1861-1867* (Series 2: The Black Military Experience). Cambridge: Cambridge University Press, 1982.

Bowen, James L., *Massachusetts in the War, 1861-1865*. Springfield, Mass.: Clark W. Bryan, 1889.

Brockett, L. P., and Mary C. Vaughan, *Woman's Work in the Civil War: A Record of Heroism, Patriotism and Patience*. Boston: R. H. Curren, 1867.

Bruce, Robert V., *Lincoln and the Tools of War*. Indianapolis: Bobbs-Merrill, 1956.

Chase, Salmon P., *Inside Lincoln's Cabinet: The Civil War Diaries of Salmon P. Chase*. Ed. by David Donald. New York: Longmans, Green, 1954.

Cole, Arthur C., *The Irrepressible Conflict, 1850-1865*. Chicago: Quadrangle Books, 1971.

Croffut, W. A., and John M. Morris, *The Military and Civil History of Connecticut during the War of 1861-65*. New York: Ledyard Bill, 1868.

Dicey, Edward, *Spectator of America*. Chicago: Quadrangle Books, 1971.

Douglass, Frederick, *Life and Times of Frederick Douglass*. New York: Pathway Press, 1941.

Fite, Emerson David, *Social and Industrial Conditions in the North during the Civil War*. New York: Macmillan, 1910.

Giddens, Paul H., *The Early Petroleum Industry*. Philadelphia: Porcupine Press, 1974.

Giddens, Paul H., ed., *Pennsylvania Petroleum, 1750-1872: A Documentary History*. Titusville: Pennsylvania Historical and Museum Commission, 1947.

Goodrich, Frank B., *The Tribute Book: A Record of the Munificence, Self-sacrifice and Patriotism of the American People during the War for the Union*. New York: Derby & Miller, 1865.

Gray, Wood, *The Hidden Civil War: The Story of the Copperheads*. New York: Viking Press, 1942.

Green, Constance McLaughlin, *Washington: Village and Capital, 1800-1878*. Princeton: Princeton University Press, 1962.

Greenbie, Marjorie Barstow, *Lincoln's Daughters of Mercy*. New York: G. P. Putnam's Sons, 1944.

Harper, Robert S., *Lincoln and the Press*. New York: McGraw-Hill, 1951.

Harris, Middleton A., et al., *The Black Book*. New York: Random House, 1974.

Hepburn, A. Barton, *A History of Currency in the United States*. New York: Augustus M. Kelley, 1967.

Hesseltine, William B., *Lincoln and the War Governors*. New York: Alfred A. Knopf, 1948.

Holbrook, Stewart H., *The Story of American Railroads*. New York: Crown Publishers, 1947.

Hubbart, Henry Clyde, *The Older Middle West, 1840-1880*. New York: D. Appleton-Century, 1936.

Katz, William Loren, ed., *Anti-Negro Riots in the North, 1863*. New York: Arno Press, 1969.

Klement, Frank L.:
The Copperheads in the Middle West. Gloucester, Mass.: Peter Smith, 1972.
The Limits of Dissent: Clement L. Vallandigham & the Civil War. Lexington: University Press of Kentucky, 1970.

Langston, John Mercer, *From the Virginia Plantation to the National Capitol*. Hartford: American Publishing, 1894.

Lanier, Henry Wysham, *A Century of Banking in New York, 1822-1922*. New York: George H. Doran, 1922.

Leach, Jack Franklin, *Conscription in the United States: Historical Background*. Rutland, Vt.: Charles E. Tuttle Publishing, 1952.

Leech, Margaret, *Reveille in Washington, 1860-1865*. New York: Harper & Row, 1941.

Lightfoot, Frederick S., ed., *Nineteenth-Century New York in Rare Photographic Views*. New York: Dover Publications, 1981.

Lindeman, Jack, ed., *The Conflict of Convictions*. Philadelphia: Chilton, 1968.

Livermore, Mary A., *My Story of the War: A Woman's Narrative of Four Years Personal Experience*. Hartford: A. D. Worthington, 1889.

Lowenfels, Walter, ed., *Walt Whitman's Civil War*. New York: Alfred A. Knopf, 1960.

McPherson, James M., *Ordeal by Fire: The Civil War and Reconstruction*. New York: Alfred A. Knopf, 1982.

Marshall, Helen E., *Dorothea Dix: Forgotten Samaritan*. New York: Russell & Russell, 1967.

Marshall, John A., *American Bastile: A History of the Illegal Arrests and Imprisonment of American Citizens during the Late Civil War*. New York: Da Capo Press, 1970.

Massey, Mary Elizabeth, *Bonnet Brigades*. New York: Alfred A. Knopf, 1966.

Maxwell, William Quentin, *Lincoln's Fifth Wheel: The Political History of the United States Sanitary Commission*. New York: Longmans, Green, 1956.

Miller, Francis Trevelyan, ed., *The Photographic History of the Civil War*. Vol. 9. New York: Review of Reviews, 1912.

Mitchell, Wesley Clair, *A History of the Greenbacks*. Chicago: University of Chicago Press, 1903.

Moss, Lemuel, *Annals of the United States Christian Commission*. Philadelphia: J. B. Lippincott, 1868.

Murdock, Eugene C.:
One Million Men: The Civil War Draft in the North. Madison: The State Historical Society of Wisconsin, 1971.
Patriotism Limited, 1862-1865: The Civil War Draft and the Bounty System. Kent, Ohio: Kent State University Press, 1967.

Myers, William Starr, *General George Brinton McClellan: A Study in Personality*. New York: D. Appleton-Century, 1934.

Naylor, Colin T., Jr., *Civil War Days in a Country Village*. Peekskill, N.Y.: Highland Press, 1961.

Nevins, Allan:
Fremont: Pathmarker of the West. Vol. 2. New York: Frederick Ungar, 1939.
John D. Rockefeller: The Heroic Age of American Enterprise. Vol. 1. New York: Charles Scribner's Sons, 1940.
The War for the Union. 4 vols. New York: Charles Scribner's Sons, 1959.

Niven, John, *Connecticut for the Union: The Role of the State in the Civil War*. New Haven: Yale University Press, 1965.

Oates, Stephen B., *With Malice toward None: The Life of Abraham Lincoln*. New York: Harper & Row, 1977.

Pleasants, Samuel Augustus, *Fernando Wood of New York*. New York: Columbia University Press, 1948.

Randall, J. G.:
Constitutional Problems under Lincoln. Urbana: University of Illinois Press, 1964.
Lincoln the President: Springfield to Gettysburg. Vol. 2. Gloucester, Mass.: Peter Smith, 1976.

Randall, J. G., and David Donald, *The Divided Union*. Boston: Little, Brown, 1961.

Reid, Whitelaw, *Ohio in the War: Her Statesmen, Her Generals, and Soldiers*. 2 vols. Cincinnati: Moore, Wilstach & Baldwin, 1868.

Shannon, Fred Albert, *The Organization and Administration of the Union Army, 1861-1865*. 2 vols. Gloucester, Mass.: Peter Smith, 1965.

Sharkey, Robert P., *Money, Class, and Party: An Economic Study of Civil War and Reconstruction*. Baltimore: Johns Hopkins Press, 1959.

Smith, George Winston, and Charles Judah, *Life in the North during the Civil War: A Source History*. Albuquerque: University of New Mexico Press, 1966.

Stampp, Kenneth M., *Indiana Politics during the Civil War*. Indianapolis: Indiana University Press, 1978.

Staudenraus, P. J., ed., *Mr. Lincoln's Washington: Selections from the Writings of Noah Brooks, Civil War Correspondent*. South Brunswick, N.J.: Thomas Yoseloff, 1967.

Sterling, Dorothy, *The Making of an Afro-American: Martin Robison Delany, 1812-1885*. Garden City: Doubleday, 1971.

Stillé, Charles J., *History of the United States Sanitary Commission*. New York: Hurd and Houghton, 1868.

Strong, George Templeton, *Diary of the Civil War, 1860-1865*. Ed. by Allan Nevins. New York: Macmillan, 1962.

Taylor, George Rogers, and Irene D. Neu, *The American Railroad Network, 1861-1890*. Cambridge: Harvard University Press, 1956.

Trollope, Anthony, *North America*. New York: Harper & Brothers, 1863.

United States War Department, *The War of the Rebellion: A Compilation of the Official Records of the Union and Confederate Armies*. Series 3, Vols. 2 and 3. Washington: Government Printing Office, 1902.

Wall, Joseph Frazier, *Andrew Carnegie*. New York: Oxford University Press, 1970.

Weber, Thomas, *The Northern Railroads in the Civil War, 1861-1865*. New York: Columbia University, 1952.

Welles, Gideon, *Diary of Gideon Welles*. Vol. 1. Boston: Houghton Mifflin, 1911.

Wormeley, Katharine Prescott, *The Other Side of War with the Army of the Potomac*. Boston: Ticknor, 1889.

Wubben, Hubert H., *Civil War Iowa and the Copperhead Movement*. Ames: Iowa State University Press, 1980.

Zornow, William Frank, *Lincoln & the Party Divided*. Norman: University of Oklahoma Press, 1954.

Other Sources

Bates, David Homer:
"Lincoln in Every-day Humor." *Century Magazine*, July 1907.
"Lincoln's Forebodings of Defeat at the Polls." *Century Magazine*, August 1907.

Belden, Marva Robins, and Thomas Graham Belden, "Kate Was Too Ambitious." *American Heritage*, August 1956.

Canup, Charles E., "Conscription and Draft in Indiana during the Civil War." *Indiana Magazine of History*, June 1914.

Dudley, Harold M., "The Election of 1864." *The Mississippi Valley Historical Review*, March 1932.

Frost, James A., "The Home Front in New York during the Civil War." *New York History*, July 1961.

Grant, Ellsworth S., "Gunmaker to the World." *American Heritage*, June 1968.

Lader, Lawrence, "New York's Bloodiest Week." *American Heritage*, June 1959.

Oates, Stephen B., "The Slaves Freed." *American Heritage*, December 1980.

Oliver, John W., "Draft Riots in Wisconsin during the Civil War." *The Wisconsin Magazine of History*, March 1919.

Shankman, Arnold, "Draft Resistance in Civil War Pennsylvania." *The Pennsylvania Magazine of History and Biography*, April 1977.

Stewart, George R., "The Prairie Schooner Got Them There." *American Heritage*, February 1962.

Thompson, William Y.:
"Sanitary Fairs of the Civil War." *Civil War History*, March 1958.
"The U.S. Sanitary Commission." *Civil War History*, June 1956.

Washburn, Wilcomb E., "Campaign Banners." *American Heritage*, October 1972.

Wibberley, Leonard Patrick O'Connor, "The Coming of the Green." *American Heritage*, August 1958.

Winslow, Cleveland, Letter to G. K. Warren Describing New York Draft Riots, August 7, 1863. Gouverneur K. Warren Papers, New York State Museum, Albany, New York.

INDEX

Numerals in italics indicate an illustration of the subject mentioned.

A

Academy of Music, *53, 141*
Agriculture: exports, 63; production expansion, 2, 20, 56, 62-63; women in production, 62
Alcoholic-beverages industry, 67, 72
Altoona conference, 143
American Railroad Journal, 66
Andrew, John A., 39, 143
Ann Arbor, Michigan, *24-25*
Antietam, Battle of, 39, 93
Aqueduct Bridge, *18-19*
Armour, Philip, 79
Arms production, 57, 66, 67-69; fraud in, 73
Arrests, 27, *31*, 32
Artillery weapons, *10-11*
Atlanta, capture of, 158
Atlantic, 43
Atlantic & Great Western Railroad, 65
Austin, Nevada Territory, 116

B

Baltimore & Ohio Railroad, 65, 73
Banking industry, 78
Banks, Nathaniel, 75-76
Barnett, T. J., 142
Barnum, Phineas T., 53
Barnum's American Museum, *52*
Barton, Clara, 128
Beckwith, Dr., 89, 92
Beecher, Henry Ward, 151
Bellows, Henry, 122, 127
Bennett, James Gordon, 144, 158
Bickerdyke, Mary Ann, 128-130
Blacks: children, care of, *104*, 105; hostility toward, 35, 99-103, 105, *106-107*, 108-110; immigrants, relations with, 40; living conditions, 102; lynchings, 35; murders of, 103, *107*, 108, 110; percentage of population, 21; public opinion on, 35-36. *See also* Black troops; Emancipation; Slavery
Black troops, *100*; number enlisted, 101; recruitment of, 36, 95, *100*, 101; 20th U.S. Colored Troops, 4; 26th U.S. Colored Troops, *101*; 54th and 55th Massachusetts Infantry Regiments, 101
Blackwell, Elizabeth, 120
Blair, Montgomery, 29

Blake, Lyman, 66
Blanchard, Jonathan, 71
Boon, Tracey G., 133
Booth, Edwin, 53
Boston & Worcester Railroad, 79
Boston draft riot, 110
Boston Review, 71
Bounty system, 87, 89, *94-95*, 98
Bridgeport, Connecticut, *22*
Bridgeport *Farmer*, 20, 22
Brooklyn, New York, *48;* civil disorders, 102-103; relief work in, *138, 140*
Brooklyn *Daily Eagle*, 77
Brooks Brothers, *107*
Brough, John, 95, 150-151
Browning, Orville, 146
Bryan, T. B., 135
Bryant, William Cullen, 151, 153
Bucklin, Sophronia, 127
Buffalo, New York, 103
Bull Run, First Battle of, 87
Burlington County, New Jersey, 100
Burnside, Ambrose, 26, 30-31
Butler, Andrew J., 75
Butler, Benjamin, 75

C

California, disloyalty in, 29
Camden & Amboy Railroad, 79
Cameron, Simon: and relief agencies, 120; as Secretary of War, 73
Camp William Penn, Pennsylvania, 101
Capitol building, *15*
Carnegie, Andrew, 70-71, *79*
Castle Garden, *50*
Casualties, 93; evacuation of, 124, *125;* treatment of, *17*, 87-89, 116, 120-122, 126-129, *130-131. See also* Hospitals; Medical Department; Nurses; United States Sanitary Commission
Central Park, *54-55*
Chandler, Zachariah, 146
Chase, Kate, *150*
Chase, Salmon P., *58, 148;* and currency supply, 58; on emancipation, 39, 58; Lincoln, relations with, 146-147, 154; presidential ambitions, 150, 152; resignation, 147, 154; Seward, rivalry with, 146-147; and war financing, 56-58. *See also* Treasury Department
Chester *Picket Guard*, 29
Chicago, Illinois: civil disorders, 99;

construction boom, 23; population growth, 22; relief work in, 133
Chicago *Times*, 30-31
Chicago *Tribune*, 30, 79, 133, 146
Children, military playthings of, *112-113*
Cincinnati, Ohio: business decline, 57; civil disorder, 35, 103; German influence in, 21
Cincinnati *Gazette*, 63
Cities, population shift to, 20, 22-23
City Point, Virginia, *100*, 132
Civil disorders, 86; in Connecticut, 20, *22;* in Illinois, 99; incidence, 23; in Massachusetts, 29, 110; in Michigan, 103; in New York City, 40, 53, 103-110; in New York State, 102-103; in Ohio, 27, 35, 103; in Pennsylvania, 99; in Wisconsin, 35, 92
Civil rights, restrictions on, 20, 29-34
Clergymen in relief work, *17, 131*
Cleveland, Ohio, relief work in, 125-126
Clothing industry, 66, 76
Coal production, 57
Collamer, Jacob, 147
Colorado Territory, 21-22
Colt, Samuel, 68
Colt firearms factory, *68-69*
Columbia Oil Company, 70-71
Columbus *Crisis*, 29
Comstock Lode, 71
Conglomerates, growth of, 78-79
Congress: and Cabinet changes, 146-147; Lincoln, relations with, 142-147; and reconstruction, 154. *See also* Radical Republicans
Conkling, Roscoe, 98
Connecticut, disloyalty in, 20
Connecticut troops, 11th Infantry Regiment, 119
Conscription. *See* Draft; Recruitment
Construction programs, 23
Copperheads: and draft, 149; and emancipation, 39, 149; and peace movement, 24, 28, *33*, 149, 151
Corcoran, W. W., 16
Cornish, Virgil, 117
Cortland, New York, 95
Cortland *Democrat*, 95
Cotton, speculation in, 73
Country Gentleman, 22-23
Cox, Samuel S., 103
Crawford Democrat, 102

Crime rates, 23
Cummings, Alexander, 73
Currency supply, 45, 57-59, *60-61*
Curtin, Andrew, 151

D

Daniel Webster, 131
Davis, David, 153-154
Davis, Henry Winter, 154
Dayton, Ohio, civil disorder in, 27
Dayton *Daily Journal*, 27
De Forest, John W., 36
Delany, Martin Robison, *100*, 101
Democratic Party, factionalism in, 24, 142, 155
Derrickson, Ann, 108
Detroit, Michigan, *96-97*
Dicey, Edward, 21, 34-35, 102
Dickens, Charles, 48
Dickinson, Emily, 89
Diseases: control, 124-125; incidence, 23
Dix, Dorothea, 127-128
Douglass, Frederick, *100;* on blacks as Americans, 35; on blacks as soldiers, 101; on emancipation, 37; on race relations, 102
Draft: commutations, 70-71, 88-89, 93, 95, 105, 110; corruption in, 89-92, 98-99; evasions and exemptions, 86, 89-91, *92-93*, 95, 98-99, 110; instituted, 31, 86, 89, 93-95; lottery selection, *87;* opposition to, 20, 31, 86, 92, 95, 98-105, *106-107*, 108, 110, 149; troop quotas, 93, 95, *98*, 110; troops raised, 92, 110. *See also* Recruitment
Drake, Edwin, 67, *70*
Dubuque *Herald*, 32

E

Eastman, Arthur, 73
Elections, national, 142-144, 146, 149-155, 158-159, 161; campaign memorabilia, *156-157. See also* Soldiers; Voters, restrictions on
Ellsworth, Elmer, *139*
Emancipation: opposition to, 108-109, 149-150; proclaimed, *38*, 39; propaganda for, *37;* public opinion on, 20, 36-37, 39. *See also* Blacks; Slavery
Emerson, Ralph Waldo, 36, 39, 86
Emigration, 23, *64-65*
Erie Railroad, 65

174